EVERY DAY

WITH

JESUS

~

Devotional Collection

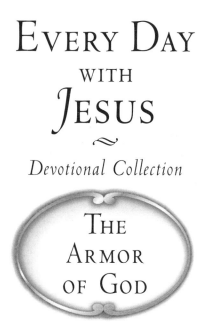

THE
ARMOR
OF GOD

Two Full Months of Daily Readings by

SELWYN HUGHES

B&H
PUBLISHING GROUP

Nashville, Tennessee

CONTENTS

INTRODUCTION

Many Christians enter each day unaware that they are being watched and opposed by a powerful enemy. Many who *do* accept this reality, however, live in unnecessary *fear* of their foe, not knowing or applying the weapons of warfare entrusted to all believers by the Lord Jesus Christ.

Throughout this book of devotional readings, we will explore in rich detail the six pieces of spiritual armor described in Ephesians 6—both the offensive and defensive measures we have been given by God, tools which enable us to protect our spirits while advancing in our walk with Christ.

It is not an inconsistency to attach the elements of warfare to a faith which promotes and pursues peace, for oftentimes peace must be carved from the hard rock of temptation, trials, difficulty, and despair. The "fiery darts" of our enemy cannot be withstood by either retreat or denial. In order to press forth unto victory in our Christian experience, we must take up our positions, put on our armor, and launch into each day with the confidence that our faith is sure and our Father supreme.

May you never be deceived into believing that Satan has slowed in his hot pursuit of your affections. But may you ever know that your God will supply all your need—even your need for certain victory in battle.

A CALL TO ARMS

"For our struggle is not against flesh and blood." (6:12)

~

We begin now a detailed study of Ephesians 6:10-20, which concerns the spiritual protection that is available to every Christian when doing battle with the devil. All those who have committed their lives to Jesus Christ know (or should know) that the kingdoms of God and the devil are locked together in mortal combat. And Christians, whether they like it or not, are thrust right onto the cutting edge of that conflict.

Many Christians are pacifists when it comes to the matter of *earthly* warfare, but no one can be a pacifist when it comes to the matter of *spiritual* warfare. Once we enlist in the army of God, we are then expected to train in the art of offensive and defensive spiritual warfare. At certain times and occasions in the Christian life, we find ourselves in a battle that demands fierce hand-to-hand combat with the forces of darkness, and unless we know how to handle these trying situations, we shall easily be overthrown.

The Bible shows us that the devil and his minions are bitter enemies of God, but because they are powerless against the

Almighty, they turn their concentrated attention on those who are His followers—you and me. Did you notice how many times the word *against* appears in the passage before us today (Eph. 6:10-13)? It occurs six times in all, showing that when anyone comes over to the side of Jesus Christ, they are immediately identified as being *for* God and *against* the devil. There can be no compromise on this issue, no peaceful coexistence pact. To be for God is to be against the devil.

PRAYER

Gracious and loving Father, help me get my perspectives clear. Train me in the art of spiritual warfare so that I will be able to resist every onslaught of the devil and come through every conflict victoriously. In Jesus' name. Amen.

~

FURTHER STUDY

2 Cor. 10:1-5; 1 Tim. 1:18; 6:12
What does Paul say about our weapons of warfare?
What was Paul's charge to Timothy?

Is There a Personal Devil?

"He was a murderer from the beginning." (8:44)

❧

Surprising as it may sound, some Christians do not believe in a personal devil. A modern-day theologian writes: "Let us put to sleep this idea of a personal devil who walks about with a pitchfork seeking to tumble people into hell. Evil is not a personality but an influence—it is just the darkness where the light ought to be."

While I agree that the picture of a personal devil walking about with a pitchfork and with horns and a tail is not to be found anywhere in Scripture, the concept of a personal devil is found *everywhere* in Scripture. One evidence of this is the fact that many of the names given to him denote his personality: Satan, deceiver, liar, murderer, accuser, tempter, prince of the power of the air, and so on. Listen to what someone has written on this subject:

> *Men don't believe in the devil now, as their fathers used to do.*
> *They reject one creed because it's old, for another because it's new.*
> *But who dogs the steps of the toiling saint,*
> *who spreads the net for his feet?*

Who sows the tares in the world's broad fields
    where the Savior sows His wheat?
They may say the devil has never lived;
    they may say the devil has gone,
But simple people would like to know—
    who carries his business on?

Take it from me, whether or not you believe in the devil, he most certainly believes in you.

PRAYER

Father, help me see that it is to Satan's advantage for me not to believe in him. Then he can do his evil work unresisted. Over these coming weeks, unfold to me the strategies I need to overcome him. In Christ's name I ask it. Amen.

∽

FURTHER STUDY

2 Cor. 11:1-14; 1 Thess. 3:5; 1 Pet. 5:8; Rev. 12:10
What are some of the guises in which Satan comes to us?
How does Peter describe him?

INFLUENCE OR INTELLIGENCE?

FOR READING AND MEDITATION—
MATTHEW 4:1–11

"Jesus said to him, 'Away from me, Satan!
For it is written . . .'" (4:10)

∼

As we have said, some of the names given to the devil in Scripture show him to be a real personality. But if more proof is required, then consider the passage that is before us today. Jesus is seen here in direct confrontation with the devil, even engaging in conversation with him. Some liberal theologians explain this in these terms: Christ was having a conversation with the dark thoughts that arose within His nature, so any "devil" that was present was subjective, not objective.

If we allow the notion that Christ had dark thoughts within His nature, then the whole scheme of redemption tumbles like a pack of cards, for a Savior who is not perfect could never fully atone for our sins. As Dr. Handley Moule puts it: "A Savior who is not perfect is like a bridge broken at one end and is not a reliable passage of access." Once we try to get around Scripture, we create endless difficulties for ourselves and finish up looking foolish. Far better to accept the Bible as it stands and believe its testimony on everything.

It is actually to Satan's advantage to get us to believe that he is not a personal being, for if there is no personal devil, there can be no personal resistance. Don't allow yourself to be deceived into thinking that the term *devil* is a synonym for the evil influence that is in the world. The devil is more than an evil influence; he is an evil intelligence. Only when we recognize this fact will we be motivated to take effective steps to resist him.

PRAYER

Father, help me see that the first step in spiritual warfare is to "know the enemy." For until I know and understand my enemy, I will not be able to defeat him. Deepen my knowledge of these important truths, I pray. In Jesus' name. Amen.

~

FURTHER STUDY

1 John 3:1-8; Heb. 2:14; John 12:30-31
Why was Jesus made manifest?
What did He declare?

THE DEVIL'S CLEFT FOOT

FOR READING AND MEDITATION—
ISAIAH 14:9–15 & EZEKIEL 28:11–19

"You said in your heart . . . 'I will make myself like the Most High.'" (Isa. 14:13-14)

❧

New Christians often ask: just who is the devil, and where did he come from? The 17th-century poet John Donne wrote that there were two things he could not fathom: "Where all the past years are, and who cleft the devil's foot." The origin, existence, and activities of the devil have always been among man's most puzzling problems. The books of Isaiah and Ezekiel give us a very clear picture, however, of what someone has called "The Rise and Fall of the Satanic Empire."

Jesus said one day to His disciples: "I saw Satan falling from heaven as a flash of lightning" (Luke 10:18, TLB). Before he was known as the devil, Satan was called Lucifer and was created as a perfect angelic being. The passages before us today show him to have been a beautiful and morally perfect being. "You were the perfection of wisdom and beauty . . . perfect in all you did from the day you were created" (Ezek. 28:12, 15, TLB).

Upright, beautiful, brilliant, and with an enormous capacity for achievement, the angel Lucifer was entrusted by God with the highest of all the offices in the interstellar universe: "You were anointed as a guardian cherub. . . . You were on the holy mount of God" (Ezek. 28:14). In his heart, however, arose a rebellious thought: "I will be like the Most High" (Isa. 14:14, NKJV). Five times that phrase "I will" is used in this passage. Those two little words—"I will"—reveal what lies behind the awful blight of sin—a created will coming into conflict with the will of the Creator.

PRAYER

O Father, now that I see the real issue that lies behind sin—a created will colliding with the will of the Creator—help me constantly to align my will with Your will. In Jesus' name I ask it. Amen.

~

FURTHER STUDY

Prov. 16:1-18; 26:12; 3:7
What comes before a fall?
What attitude should we guard against?

SATANIC FORCES

*"Angels who did not keep their positions
of authority . . . he has kept in darkness,
bound with everlasting chains." (1:6)*

~

We saw in the previous reading that the devil was created as
a wise and morally perfect being (then known as Lucifer) who
aspired to take over the throne of God and thus usurp the position of his Creator. Once that happened, Lucifer was expelled
from heaven, together with the other angels who had sensed
and shared his rebellious attitude. This is the fall from heaven
that Jesus told His disciples He had witnessed.

Since his fall from heaven, Satan, apparently losing little of
his administrative skill, has marshaled these fallen angels (now
known as demons) into a hostile force to work against God and
His creation. We do not know just how many angels fell with
Satan, but doubtless it must have been a colossal number.
When Jesus once asked a demoniac: "What is your name?"
(Luke 8:30), the demons answered: "Legion." If they were
telling the truth, the man was controlled by thousands of
demons. A Roman legion contained six thousand men!

It is little wonder, then, that the apostle Paul warned the Ephesians that they were involved in a tremendous spiritual conflict: "We are not fighting against people made of flesh and blood, but against persons without bodies—the evil rulers of the unseen world, those mighty satanic beings and great evil princes of darkness who rule this world" (Eph. 6:12, TLB).

One of America's founding fathers said: "If men will not be governed by God, then they will be ruled by tyrants." How sad that people actually choose to be governed by Satan rather than by God.

PRAYER

O God my Father, I am so thankful that I have left the tyranny and rule of Satan to come under the sway of Your eternal and everlasting kingdom. May I come more and more under its sway hour by hour and day by day. In Jesus' name I pray. Amen.

⁓

FURTHER STUDY

Luke 10:1-19; Psa. 44:5; Rom. 8:31
What event did Jesus witness?
What power did He give to His disciples?

DANGER—THE DEVIL AT WORK

FOR READING AND MEDITATION—
I PETER 5:1–11

*"Your enemy the devil prowls around
like a roaring lion." (5:8)*

❧

A woman said to me once: "I think you are giving too much credit to the devil. He is such an insignificant person compared to God that we ought not even mention his name." In one way I can sympathize with this view, for when you listen to some Christians talk, you get the impression that they have a small God and a big devil.

It would be unrealistic to think, however, that we can go through life without coming into direct contact with Satan and his forces. What is even more unrealistic is to think that many (though certainly not all) of the problems which confront us day by day have no devilish strategy behind them.

Satan is responsible for more of our individual woes and international wars, our crime and violence, our human sorrow, sickness, and death than we may believe. The late Dr. Martyn Lloyd-Jones said: "I am certain that one of the main causes of the ill state of the church today is the fact that the devil is being forgotten. . . . We are ignorant of this great objective fact—the being, the existence of the devil, the adversary, the accuser, and his fiery darts."

Does the thought of doing battle with the devil frighten you? Then heed the words of Corrie ten Boom, who said: "The fear of the devil is most likely from the devil himself." God has given us all the protection we need to defend ourselves against the attacks of Satan, and when we know how to avail ourselves of this protection, we will no longer be afraid of the devil. Rather, he will be afraid of us.

PRAYER

O God, as I go deeper into this subject, I am becoming increasingly aware of the intensity of the spiritual battle in which I am engaged. Dispel every fear that may arise in me and show me the way to power and victory. In Jesus' name. Amen.

≈

FURTHER STUDY

2 Cor. 2:1-11; 11:3; 2 Thess. 2:9
What did Paul say about his knowledge of the devil?
What was his reason?

OUR ONLY PROTECTION

FOR READING AND MEDITATION—
EPHESIANS 6:11–18

"Put on the whole armor of God, that you may be able to stand against the wiles of the devil." (6:11, NKJV)

~

We concentrate now on two vital issues: the armor of God is our *only protection* against the wiles of Satan, but it will do us no good unless we avail ourselves of it *in its entirety.*

In considering the first of these matters, we must constantly keep before us the fact that such is the might and power of Satan that nothing apart from the armor of God will protect us from his onslaughts. Mark this and mark it well, for there are many Christians who have tried to stand against Satan in their own strength and have found themselves not victors but victims. One of the "wiles" of Satan is to get us to believe that we can resist him in our own strength. But the moment we think this—we are finished!

In my time I have seen many believers lulled by Satan into thinking that their long experience in the faith and their understanding of Christian doctrine were all they needed in order to be protected from satanic attack. But they found to their great cost that this was inadequate and insufficient. We never live more dangerously than when we depend on our spiritual experience and understanding to protect us from the fiery darts of the enemy.

One thing and one thing only can protect us from the attacks of Satan, and that is the spiritual armor which God has provided to His people. In the devil, you see, we are dealing with a foe who is inferior in power only to the Almighty Himself. Therefore, nothing less than the protection that God provides is adequate for our need.

PRAYER

O Father, I need to get this matter straight,
for I see that if my dependence is on anything other
than You, then I am sunk. Drive this truth deep
into my spirit this day. In Jesus' name. Amen.

~

FURTHER STUDY

Rom. 13:1-12; 1 Thess. 5:8; 2 Tim. 2:4
What are we to put aside?
What are we to put on?

"WOBBLY CHRISTIANS"

FOR READING AND MEDITATION—
ROMANS 13:8–14

*"So let us put aside the deeds of darkness
and put on the armor of light." (13:12)*

~

The armor of God will not do us any good unless it is worn
in its entirety. We must put on the whole armor of God, not
just a few of the pieces we think are most suitable for us.

This again is something of crucial importance. If we are to
be steadfast soldiers in the Lord's army, if we are to avoid
becoming what John Stott calls "wobbly Christians who have
no firm foothold in Christ," then we must put on the entire
equipment which God provides for us. We cannot—we dare
not—select parts of the armor and say: "I don't really like the
helmet of salvation, but I don't mind wearing the breastplate of
righteousness." You can do that, of course, but if you do, then
you must know exactly what will happen to you—you will be
overcome by Satan. The moment you say: "I need the breastplate, but I don't need the helmet," you are defeated. You need
it all—the whole armor of God.

You see, our understanding of what is involved in spiritual
defense against Satan is extremely inadequate. We just don't

have sufficient knowledge of what is involved. It is God alone who knows our enemy, and it is God alone who knows exactly how to protect us so that we remain firm and steadfast when Satan and his forces hurl themselves against us. So learn this lesson now before going any further—every single piece of God's armor is essential, and to select some and leave out the others is to take the route to failure and defeat.

PRAYER

O God, deliver me from the attitude of pride that seeks to put my ideas ahead of Your ideas. You know more about what I need to protect me from the enemy than I do. Help me ever to trust Your judgment. In Jesus' name I ask it. Amen.

~

FURTHER STUDY

2 Cor. 6:1-10; Phil. 1:27; 1 Pet. 5:9

What was a necessary requirement for Paul's ministry?

What are we called to do?

THE BELT OF TRUTH

FOR READING AND MEDITATION—
PSALM 119:145–160

"Yet you are near, O LORD,
and all your commands are true." (119:151)

~

Paul, in listing the six main pieces of a soldier's equipment, illustrated the six main ways by which we can defend ourselves against the power of Satan—*truth, righteousness, steadfastness, faith, salvation,* and *the Word of God.*

Most commentators believe that the reason why Paul chose these six pieces of armor to describe the Christian's protective system against satanic attack was because he was chained to a soldier as he wrote the letter (Eph. 6:20). Although it is probably unlikely that the soldier standing guard in prison would have worn the full armor of an infantryman on the battlefield, the sight of him would have kindled Paul's imagination.

The list begins with the *belt of truth.* Why, we ask ourselves, does the apostle start with such a seemingly insignificant item? Why did he not begin with one of the bigger and more important pieces of equipment, such as the breastplate, the shield, or the sword of the Spirit? The order in which these pieces are given to us is an inspired order, and if we change the order we make our position extremely perilous. For example, the reason why many Christians fail to wield the sword of the Spirit effectively is because they have not first girded their waist with truth. If we reverse the order, we succeed only in weakening our spiritual defense.

It is very important that we grasp this. Girding our waist with truth is always the place to start whenever we are under satanic attack. If we don't start right, then we will not finish right. We cannot do battle with the devil until we first gird our waists with truth.

PRAYER

Gracious and loving Father, help me to absorb this thought into my inner being this day so that it will stay with me for the rest of my life: I cannot do battle with the devil until I first gird my waist with truth. Amen.

~

FURTHER STUDY

2 Pet. 1:1-12; Prov. 23:23; 3 John 1-4
In what are we to be established?
In what did John rejoice?

23

THE POWER OF TRUTH

"Surely you desire truth in the inner parts." (51:6)

❧

We cannot do battle with the devil until we have girded our waists with truth. Girding the waist was always a symbol of readiness to fight. That is why this comes first. The officers in the Roman army wore short skirts, very much like a Scottish kilt. Over this they had a cloak or tunic which was secured at the waist with a girdle. When they were about to enter battle, they would tuck the tunic up under the girdle so as to leave their legs unencumbered for the fight.

What does Paul's phrase, "gird your waist with truth" really mean? What significance does it have for us today? The word *truth* can be looked at in two ways: one, *objective truth*, as it is to be found in Jesus Christ, and two, *subjective truth* as it is to be found in the qualities of honesty and sincerity. The Puritan, William Gurnall, points out that whether the word implies truth of doctrine or truth of heart, one kind of truth will not do without the other.

I believe that in Ephesians 6, Paul is emphasizing subjective truth—truth that resides in the inner being. When we are deceitful or hypocritical, or when we resort to intrigue and scheming, we are playing the devil's game. And we will never be able to beat the devil at his own game!

What Satan despises is transparent truth. He flees from it as quickly as darkness runs from the dawn. Having our waists girded with truth, then, means being possessed with truth, guided by truth, and controlled by truth. Where truth is absent, we have no power over Satan. It is as simple as that.

PRAYER

*O Father, I see that You have set standards by which
I rise or fall. When I fulfill them, I rise—when I break
them, I fall. Give me the strength I need to fulfill all Your
laws, especially the law of truth. In Jesus' name. Amen.*

FURTHER STUDY

John 8:34-45; Col. 3:9; Prov. 12:22
What can protect us from the devil?
Where should we desire truth?

THE SEARCHLIGHT OF TRUTH

FOR READING AND MEDITATION—
PSALM 139:1–24

*"Search me [thoroughly], O God, and know my heart!
Try me, and know my thoughts!" (139:23, AMPLIFIED)*

❧

We remind ourselves of what we said previously—that to
have our "waist girded with truth" means to be possessed by
truth. If we are to defend ourselves effectively against the
attacks of Satan, then truth and honesty are vital necessities.

The mental health experts tell us that being willing to face
the truth about ourselves is an important part of our growth
toward maturity. The same is true in the realm of the spiritual.
How easy it is to hide from the truth and imagine ourselves to
be truthful when really we are not.

Whatever his personal idiosyncrasies and his rebellious attitude toward Christianity, Sigmund Freud made an interesting
contribution to our understanding of human personality when
he documented with true genius the incredibly subtle ways in
which we lie to ourselves. Psychologists call them "defense
mechanisms," but a more biblical view of them would be "lying
mechanisms." We would all much prefer to be called defensive
than dishonest. But whenever we allow ourselves to be self-

deceived, we not only impede our spiritual growth—we also lower our defenses against Satan. He thrives on deception, and if he can push us toward self-deception, he maintains a definite advantage over us.

Many of us might react with horror to the suggestion that we are being dishonest, for we would not dream of doing or saying anything that was not according to the truth. Yet it is possible to be open and honest on the outside and yet hide from truth on the inside. All of us, even mature and experienced Christians, are capable of hiding from truth.

PRAYER

O Father, I see that if I am to overcome Satan, then I must know truth inwardly as well as outwardly. Search my heart today, dear Lord, and bring to the surface the things within me that are untrue. In Jesus' name I ask it. Amen.

FURTHER STUDY

2 Chron. 7:1-14; Isa. 44:20; James 1:22
What are God's people to turn from?
What does James warn against?

THREE FORMS OF DISHONESTY

FOR READING AND MEDITATION—
I JOHN 1:1–10

"If we claim to be without sin, we deceive ourselves and the truth is not in us." (1:8)

～

The suggestion that even mature Christians can inwardly resist truth might shock some, but the real issue is—is it true?

Among the popular defenses we use to resist truth, the first is *projection*. This occurs when we are to blame for something, but we project the blame onto someone else so that we can feel more comfortable about ourselves. It may sound a simple thing, but all dishonesty is destructive—even simple dishonesty.

Then take the defense of *denial*. How many times do we refuse to face the fact that we may be angry about something, and when someone says: "Why are you angry?" we reply with bristling hostility: "I'm not angry!" We fail to recognize what others can plainly see. And denial, no matter how one looks at it, is a form of inner deceit.

Another dishonest defense is *rationalization*. We are guilty of this whenever we persuade ourselves that something is what it is not. C. S. Lewis points out that when our *neighbor* does something wrong, it is obviously because he or she is "bad," while if *we* do something wrong it is only because we did not get enough sleep, or someone gave us a rough time, or our blood chemistry is at fault, and so on.

All of these defense mechanisms deprive us of inner honesty, and apart from hindering our spiritual growth (as we have said) they also lower our defenses against Satan. This is why over and over again in Scripture, we are bidden to open up to honesty. The more honest we can be, the more spiritually powerful and effective we can be.

PRAYER

Lord Jesus, help me open up to honesty. For I see that the more honest I am, the more authority I can wield over Satan. I want to be able to say, as You said: "The ruler of this world is coming, and he has nothing in me." I ask for Your name's sake. Amen.

~

FURTHER STUDY

Rev. 3:14-22; James 1:26; Gal. 6:3
How did the Laodiceans see themselves?
How did God see them?

LIFE WITHOUT TRUTH

"It is time to seek the LORD." (10:12)

~

The phrase "gird your waist with truth" clearly suggests that this is something we must do and not expect God to do for us. Clinton McLemore says: "Whenever any one of us embodies and promotes personal honesty, we are knowingly or unknowingly doing God's work."

So ask yourself: "Am I an honest person?" If there are areas of your life where you are not sure, then spend some time before God in prayer today asking Him to help you root out all dishonesty. For honesty is our first line of defense against Satan. If we are not willing to be honest, then the devil will soon disable us.

We live in an age which, generally speaking, evades the truth. We seem to take it for granted that advertisements distort, contracts contain fine print that no one draws our attention to, and professionals conceal one another's malpractice. There are few domains of life that are uncompromised, few social structures that are not tainted, few relationships that retain any semblance of wholesomeness.

The Christian church is not without blame either. Consider the endless maneuverings we've witnessed in some church boards and committees. God put the church in the world, but somehow the devil has put the world in the church.

The text atop the previous page sums up the present church situation: "It is time to seek the LORD." Am I speaking too strongly? I think not. If we don't get things straightened out at the start, then how can we hope to be victorious in the war against Satan? Always remember that sin, at its root, is a stubborn refusal to deal with truth.

PRAYER

O God, forgive us that we, Your redeemed people,
sometimes pursue our own interests and allow truth to be
dragged in the gutter. Help us, dear Lord. For without truth
we have no power. In Jesus' name we ask it. Amen.

~

FURTHER STUDY

1 Pet. 4:12-19; Rom. 12:17; Jer. 17:9
What is the natural condition of the heart?
Where must things be put right first?

THE BREASTPLATE

*"May your priests be clothed with righteousness;
may your saints sing for joy." (132:9)*

❧

We look now at the second piece of armor with which we
are to defend ourselves against the wiles of the devil—*the breastplate of righteousness.*

A soldier's breastplate generally extended from the base of
the neck to the upper part of the thighs so it would cover many
important parts of the body, in particular the heart. Some
commentators think that the word *breastplate* suggests that this
piece of equipment covered only the front of the chest and thus
gave no protection for the back. They deduce from this that a
Christian should *face* the devil and never turn his back on him,
or else he will expose a part that is unguarded. It is an interesting idea, but it must not be given too much credence, for the
soldier's breastplate often covered his back as well as his front.

What spiritual lesson *can* we draw from the "breastplate of
righteousness"? Most commentators believe that because the
soldier's breastplate primarily covered his heart, the spiritual
application of this is that in Christ we have all the protection

we need against negative or desolating feelings—the heart being seen as the focal point of the emotions.

What an exciting thought—by putting on the breastplate of righteousness, we have the spiritual resources to deal with all those debilitating feelings that tend to bring us down into despair—unworthiness, inadequacy, fear, and so on. When I mentioned this to a friend who asked me what I thought the breastplate of righteousness was for, he said: "It sounds too good to be true." I replied: "It's too good *not* to be true."

PRAYER

Gracious Lord and Master, how can I sufficiently thank You for providing a defense against this most difficult of problems— emotional distress. Show me how to apply Your truth to this part of my personality. In Jesus' name. Amen.

FURTHER STUDY

Matt. 15:10-20; Mark 7:21; Prov. 4:23; 28:9
What comes out of the heart?
How are we to guard our hearts?

CHRIST'S RIGHTEOUSNESS

FOR READING AND MEDITATION—
ROMANS 8:31–39

*"Who then will condemn us? Will Christ? No!
For he is the one who died for us."* (8:34, TLB)

～

When Paul talks about the "breastplate of righteousness," is he talking about *our* righteousness or *Christ's* righteousness?

I believe he is talking about Christ's righteousness. That is not to say, of course, that our own righteousness (our moral uprightness) is unimportant, for as Paul points out in 2 Corinthians 6:7, our righteousness can be a definite defense against Satan. In Ephesians 6, however, the emphasis is not on our righteousness in Christ, but Christ's righteousness in us.

So how does putting on the breastplate of righteousness act as a spiritual defense against the wiles of the devil? Take, for example, those people who have definitely surrendered their lives to Christ but whom Satan afflicts with a feeling that they are not good enough to be saved. Why do they have such feelings? The answer is simple—they have taken their eyes off Christ and His righteousness and have focused on themselves and their righteousness. And in doing that, they have played right into the devil's hands.

You see, the devil can find all kinds of flaws and blemishes in your righteousness, but he can find nothing wrong with the righteousness of Christ. The way to withstand an attack like this, then, is to put on the breastplate of righteousness. In other words, remind yourself and Satan that you stand not on your own merits but on Christ's. This may sound simple, even simplistic to some, but I have lived long enough to see people latch on to it and come from the depths of emotional distress to the heights of spiritual exaltation.

PRAYER

Lord Jesus, help me to latch onto it. Make it crystal clear to my spirit that although the devil can find many flaws in my righteousness, he cannot find a single flaw in Yours. I rest my case—on You. Thank You, dear Lord. Amen.

～

FURTHER STUDY

1 Cor. 1:19-31; Isa. 64:6; Phil. 3:9
What is our righteousness like?
What was Paul's declaration?

"TYRANNY OF THE OUGHTS"

"Therefore, since we have been justified by faith, we have peace with God through our Lord Jesus Christ." (5:1)

❧

The breastplate of righteousness protects us from the feeling that we are not good enough to be saved. We now look, in this devotional reading, at another feeling which Satan delights to whip up in the heart of a Christian—the feeling that we are only accepted by God when we are doing everything perfectly. This feeling gives rise to *perfectionism*—a condition which afflicts multitudes of Christians.

The chief characteristic of perfectionism is a constant over-all feeling of never doing enough to be thought well of by God. Karen Horney describes it as "the tyranny of the oughts." Here are some typical statements of those who are afflicted in this way: "I ought to do better," "I ought to have done better," "I ought to be able to do better." There is nothing wrong with wanting to do better, but in the twisted thinking of a perfectionist, a person believes that because he or she could or ought to have done better, they will not be accepted or thought well of by God. They come to believe that their acceptance by God depends on their performance. They constantly try to develop a righteousness of their own rather than resting in the righteousness which Christ has provided for them.

If you suffer from this condition, then it's time to put on your spiritual breastplate. You need to remind yourself that the way you came into the Christian life is the same way you are enabled to go on in it—by depending on Christ and His righteousness, not on yourself and your righteousness. You are not working to be saved; you are working because you are saved.

PRAYER

Lord Jesus, I see that when I stand in Your righteousness, I stand in God's smile. But when I stand in my own righteousness, I stand in God's frown. Help me move over from frown to smile. In Your dear name. Amen.

❧

FURTHER STUDY

Gal. 3; Gen. 15:6; Acts 13:39
What was the purpose of the law?
What does it mean to be "justified"?

Paul's Breastplate

For reading and meditation—
I Corinthians 15:1–11

"But by the grace of God I am what I am." (15:10)

❦

Another feeling which Satan can arouse in a heart that is unprotected by a spiritual breastplate is that of a subtle form of discouragement, in which he draws our attention to what other Christians may be saying or thinking about us.

The apostle Paul was a particular target of Satan in this respect, but see how he used the breastplate of righteousness as his spiritual defense. Paul's background was anti-Christian, and he could never get completely away from that. He had been the most hostile persecutor of the church, and he must therefore have constantly run across families whose loved ones he had put to death. Perhaps there were many who doubted his claim to be an apostle. Some commentators claim that in I Corinthians 15:9, he was replying to such an accusation.

How does Paul react to this criticism? Does he succumb to discouragement? Does he say: "What's the use of working my fingers to the bone for these unappreciative people? They don't do anything but hurl recriminations in my face!" This is what the devil would have liked him to do. But look at what he does.

He says: "By the grace of God I am what I am." Can you see what he is doing? He is using the breastplate of righteousness. He is saying, in other words: "I don't need to do anything to protect myself; what I am is what Christ has made me. I am not standing in my own righteousness, I am standing in His."

What a lesson this is in how to use the spiritual breastplate. You and I need to learn this lesson, too.

PRAYER

O God, day by day I am catching little glimpses of what You are trying to teach me—that the more I depend on Your righteousness and the less I depend on my own, the better off I will be. Help me to learn it—and learn it completely. Amen.

FURTHER STUDY

Psa. 73:1-28; 2 Cor. 5:7-21
What brought discouragement to the psalmist?
How did Paul encourage the Corinthians?

HANDLING CONFUSION

"Nothing will ever be able to separate us from the love of God demonstrated by our Lord Jesus Christ." (8:39, *TLB*)

❧

Yet another feeling which Satan delights to arouse in a heart unprotected by a spiritual breastplate is the feeling of confusion. None of us likes confusion, because it erodes our sense of competence. Satan, knowing this, steps in whenever he can to take full advantage of it.

Deep in the center of our being is a compulsive demand to be in control. And to satisfy that demand, we have to live in a predictable, understandable world. Confusion presents a serious challenge to our desire for control and is the enemy of those who demand to have clear answers for everything.

Whenever Satan sees that we are not wearing our spiritual breastplate, he comes to us and says something like this: "Look at the great problems that are all around you—earthquakes, famines, violence, cruelty to children. How can you believe in a God of love when these things are going on in the world?" Sometimes he presses home these arguments with such power that you have no clear answers.

There is only one clear answer against such assaults; it is to put on the "breastplate of righteousness." You cannot understand particular happenings; you cannot give any explanation. But you do know that the God who clothed you with His righteousness and saved you from a lost eternity must have your highest interests and those of His universe at heart. When you hold on to that, your heart is protected from despair, even if your mind struggles to comprehend what is happening. You can live in peace even though you do not know all the answers.

PRAYER

Father God, I see that I can experience security in my heart even when my mind cannot understand Your ways. Hidden in Christ and His righteousness, I am safe. I am so thankful. Amen.

❧

FURTHER STUDY

2 Tim. 1:1-7; 1 Cor. 14:33; Isa. 26:3
Where does our peace stem from?
Where does confusion come from?

SATAN—ANGEL OF LIGHT

*"He who began a good work in you will
carry it on to completion." (1:6)*

∼

Yet another feeling which the devil delights to arouse in an unguarded heart is the feeling that God does not love us. He usually times his attack to coincide with those moments when everything is going wrong and we are beset by all kinds of difficulties. Then he whispers in our ear: "Do you still believe that God is love?"

When you respond by saying that you do, he transforms himself into an angel of light and tries another of his deceitful tactics. "Well," he says, "it is obvious that He does not love you, for if He did, then He would not allow you to go through these difficult situations."

There is only one protection against such an assault; it is to put firmly in place the "breastplate of righteousness." Nothing else will avail at this point. You must point him to the truth of Romans 8:28—"We know that in all things God works for the good of those who love him." Paul does not say "we understand," but "we know."

This brings you directly to the theme of justification by faith, which is in fact the righteousness of Christ. You rest on this established truth, and that is all you need. You must say to yourself: "He would never have clothed me with His righteousness if He had not also set His love upon me and saved me. I will have courage. I do not know what is happening to me now. I cannot fathom it. But if He has begun His work in me, then I know He will go on to complete it."

PRAYER

O God, what wondrous power there is in Your Word. I can feel it doing me good even as I read and ponder it. Give me a greater knowledge of Your Word, for only through its truth can I maintain an advantage over the devil. Amen.

FURTHER STUDY

Jer. 31:1-3; Eph. 2:1-7; 3:16-19; Rom. 5:8
How has God demonstrated His love?
What was Paul's desire for the Ephesians?

REJECTED BY GOD?

*"If we confess our sins, he . . . will forgive us our sins
and purity us from all unrighteousness." (1:9)*

❧

Another feeling which the devil likes to arouse in an
unguarded heart is the feeling that when we have committed a
sin, we will be rejected by God and have to forfeit our salvation.
The Hebrew name "Satan" means "adversary," and the Greek
name for "devil" means "slanderer." This gives us a pretty
good idea of the nature of the Evil One. He is never happier
than when he is engaged in pointing the finger of scorn at us
whenever we have failed.

It is part of the doctrine of the church that a Christian may
sometimes fall into sin. We are saved, but we are still fallible.
God forbid that we should fall into sin, but when we do, we
must remember that we have "an advocate with the Father,
Jesus Christ the righteous" (I John 2:1).

You can be sure, however, that when you fall into sin, the
devil will come to you and say: "You were forgiven when you
became a Christian because you sinned in ignorance, but now
that you are a Christian, you have sinned against the light.

There can be no forgiveness for you now because of what you have done. You are lost—forever!"

The answer to this, as with all of Satan's accusations, is to put on the "breastplate of righteousness." You must remind him that God's righteousness not only covers us at our salvation but continues to cover us for time and eternity. Never allow the devil to use a particular sin to call into question your whole standing before God. This is something that has been settled in heaven, not in the debating chamber of the devil.

PRAYER

My Father and my God, my heart overflows at the revelation of Your full and free forgiveness. Help me not to take it for granted but to take it with gratitude. In Jesus' name I pray. Amen.

❧

FURTHER STUDY

Isa. 55:1-7; 43:25; Eph. 1:7–8; Acts 13:38
What does God do when He blots out our sin?
How does the Lord respond when we return to Him?

THE SHOES OF PEACE

*"Stand firm in one spirit, contending as one man
for the faith of the gospel" (1:27)*

∾

We come now to the third piece of armor—having our feet
shod "with the readiness that comes from the gospel of peace"
(Eph. 6:15).

Shoes are absolutely essential to a soldier. If he were bare-
foot, the rough ground would tear his feet to pieces and would
soon render him unfit for duty. But with a stout pair of shoes,
he is ready to face anything that may come.

Markus Barth, a Bible commentator, writes that a Roman
soldier in Paul's day would have worn not so much a shoe as a
sandal. They were known as *caligae* (half boots). This type of
footware was marked by "heavy studded leather soles and were
tied to the ankles or shins with more or less ornamental straps."
These equipped the soldier for a solid stance and prevented his
feet from slipping or sliding.

What is the spiritual application of all this? What did the
apostle Paul have in mind when he penned the words: "Stand
. . . having . . . shod your feet with the preparation of the gospel

of peace"? (NKJV). The New English Bible brings home the point of the passage in a most effective way: "Let the shoes on your feet be the gospel of peace, to give you firm footing." The shoes we are to put on are the gospel of peace—the tried and tested truths of the gospel—and their purpose is to prevent us from slipping and sliding when we do battle with our wily and nimble adversary, the devil.

What are you like when under attack from Satan? Firm and resolute? Or unsteady and unsure?

PRAYER

O Father, I see that if I am to stand firm and resolute
when under enemy attack, my feet must be securely shod.
Show me what is expected of me, dear Lord—and
help me apply it. In Jesus' name I pray. Amen.

~

FURTHER STUDY

Psa. 40:1-5; 1 Sam. 2:9; Isa. 52:1-7
What was the psalmist's testimony?
Is this your testimony?

DON'T MISS THE POINT

"Do your best to present yourself to God as one approved . . . who correctly handles the word of truth." (2:15)

~

There are some who claim that having our "feet shod with the preparation of the gospel of peace" means that we should always be ready to carry the gospel to others. That interpretation certainly fits in with Romans 10:15: "How beautiful are the feet of those who preach the gospel of peace" (NKJV), but this is not, in my opinion, what Paul had in mind when he wrote the words of Ephesians 6:15.

In Ephesians 6 the apostle is dealing with one thing only—the Christian's engagement with the devil. He said: "We do not wrestle against flesh and blood, but against principalities, against powers . . ." (v. 12, NKJV). His purpose is to show us how to stand against the "wiles" of the devil. Although Paul was an evangelist with a strong evangelistic spirit, he was not thinking here of evangelizing, vital though it is. He was rather picturing a Christian who is under attack by Satan, warning us that unless our feet are firmly shod, we can easily be knocked down and disabled.

Those who claim that the phrase "the readiness of the gospel of peace" relates to evangelism miss the point of his exposition. No one would deny the importance of always being ready to share Christ with others, but the readiness to which Paul is referring here is the readiness to stand firm on the truths of the gospel. In other words, he is saying: Don't get into a fight with the devil in your bare feet. Make sure you are well shod, for if you are not, he will most certainly get the better of you.

PRAYER

O Father, I am so grateful that You breathed into Your servant
Paul to write these illuminating words. They are inspired,
for they inspire me. Continue to teach me, dear Lord.
I am hungry for more and more of Your truth. Amen.

❧

FURTHER STUDY

Psa. 119:97-105; Isa. 40:8; 1 Pet. 1:23-25
How did the psalmist view God's Word?
Why is God's Word a sure foundation?

THE IRREDUCIBLE MINIMUM

FOR READING AND MEDITATION—
2 CORINTHIANS 1:12–24

*"For no matter how many promises God has made,
they are 'Yes' in Christ." (1:20)*

~

It is time now to face some very personal and pointed questions. Do you believe the Bible is the Word of God, divinely and uniquely inspired and reliable in all it affirms? Do you believe that Jesus Christ is the Son of God, born of a virgin, and the only way to God? Do you believe that He was crucified for your sins, raised again on the third day, and is now sitting on the right hand of God?

I could go on raising more questions, but the ones I have mentioned are what I consider to be the irreducible minimum of Christianity. In other words, these are the basic truths of the gospel, and if you don't take your stand on these truths, then you cannot call yourself a Christian.

This is what is meant by having your feet shod with the preparation of the gospel of peace—that you are ready to stand for the authority of Scripture, the deity of Christ, His substitutionary death, His resurrection from the dead, and His return to earth in power and glory.

Do you know where you stand on these matters? Are you sure of your spiritual position? How can you fight the enemy if you do not know what you believe? As I write, some of the daily newspapers here in Britain are calling on church leaders to give a spiritual lead. But many of our leaders do not have a high view of Scripture. How can they give a lead when they don't know where they are going? They don't know where they stand, and no one else knows either.

PRAYER

*O Father, Your Word promises to be a lamp to our feet
and a light for our path. Bring those whose feet are slipping
and sliding in the faith back to an unshakeable confidence
in Your gospel. In Jesus' name I ask it. Amen.*

∾

FURTHER STUDY

2 Pet. 1; Col. 2:7; 1 Cor. 3:11

Why are we given so many great and precious promises?
What should our foundation be?

FOR NEW CHRISTIANS

*"Stand firm and hold to the teachings
we passed on to you." (2:15)*

❧

Christians need to stand with their feet shod with the preparation of the gospel of peace. The moment we begin to compromise on the Word of God and the great truths of the gospel, we shall not only slide in the understanding of our faith but also in its practice.

Permit me to say a word to those who have been in the Christian life for just a short time. Now that you are a Christian, take your stand unflinchingly on the Lord's side. When you meet your old friends—those you used to hang around with in the days before you came to know the Lord—and they propose that you go on doing the things you used to do which you know are not in harmony with God's Word, then be resolute and refuse. Take a firm stand, and watch that you do not slip toward them. Have your feet shod with the preparation of the gospel of peace.

The first thing that strikes everyone who comes into the Christian life is that it is entirely different from one's former life. You must determine to take your stand with Jesus Christ, and when others tempt you, say: "I cannot betray my Lord. I am bound to Him for all eternity. My feet are shod and I am not moving." You have to know what you believe and be resolute and determined to stand for it—come what may. If I had not done this in the days following my conversion to Christ, then I would have forfeited an adventure that has taken me deeper and deeper into God.

PRAYER

O God, how can I have faith in You unless I have faith in the words You have spoken to me in the Bible? Help me stand firm in the faith—today and every day. In Jesus' name. Amen.

~

FURTHER STUDY

Gal. 5:1-13; Phil. 1:27; 1 Pet. 5:7-11
What did Paul say to the Galatians?
How should we conduct ourselves?

A SPIRITUAL ADVENTURE

"The LORD said to Gideon, 'With the three hundred men that lapped I will save you.'" (7:7)

❧

I have selected this passage today because it illustrates an important point: God is looking for people who will "stand." When the hosts of Midian came against the Israelites, Gideon gathered together a large army of 32,000 men. Then God reduced them to a mere handful. Of the 32,000, there were only three hundred whom God could trust. He saw that they were men who would stand and never quit, so He dismissed the rest. And with just a small army of three hundred, He proceeded to discomfit and rout the Midianites.

God has always done His greatest work in and through a comparatively small number of people. This is why, when it comes to spiritual victories, we forget the idea of numbers. What God wants is men and women who are prepared to "stand," whose feet are "shod with the preparation of the gospel of peace." He will not entrust great responsibility to people whom He knows will not "stand," for that would be an exercise in fruitlessness.

Are you standing for God—in the environment in which God has put you? Or, are you *ready* to stand? You cannot stand until you are prepared to stand. It begins with a firm attitude which then issues into resolute action. As in Gideon's day, the Lord is looking for people who will take their stand on His Word, come what may, and commit themselves to doing what He asks even though they may not feel like it or see the sense of it. Are you such a one? If you are, then I predict that ahead of you is an exciting spiritual adventure.

PRAYER

O God, help me not to miss the highest because of my spiritual unpreparedness. Help me to be ready for all that You have for me—even before I see it. In Jesus' name. Amen.

~

FURTHER STUDY

Gal. 6:1-9; 1 Cor. 15:58; Eph. 4:15
What is the result of remaining steadfast?
What can hinder our spiritual success?

PEACE TO THE END

"Let the peace of God rule in your hearts."
(3:15, NKJV)

❧

Why the phrase "the gospel of peace"? Well, the Gospel is first and foremost a message about peace. We first experience peace *with* God, and then we experience the peace *of* God.

A soldier in battle has to be certain about a number of things, or else he will be distracted and become an easy prey for the enemy. He needs to be certain that he is fighting in a just war, that his commander is a wise strategist, and that he has the constant support of those under whose authority he fights. He needs to know also that his loved ones are being cared for and that they are being protected by a defense force.

So, too, the Christian soldier has to be certain about his relationship with God, the truth and reliability of the Bible, the resources that are available to him, and so on. How can his heart be at peace if he is not assured of these things?

It is at this point that we Christians have an advantage over every other soldier, for not only are we led by the wisest military strategist in the universe, but we have inside information on how the battle against Satan will end—we win! We would never be able to stand against the "wiles" of the devil unless we enjoyed peace with God—and the peace *of* God. Even in the midst of the hottest conflict, we know that although the devil may win some of the battles, he will most definitely lose the war. If we have peace about the outcome, then we can have peace all the way—period.

PRAYER

O Father, I see so clearly that if I have doubts about You or about my salvation, then I will not be able to fight the enemy. I shall have to spend the whole time struggling with myself. But there are no doubts. I have peace with You and peace within. I am so thankful. Amen.

FURTHER STUDY

Phil. 4:1-7; Psa. 29:11; John 16:33; Rom. 14:17
What keeps our hearts and minds?
How does this relate to battle?

THE SHIELD OF FAITH

*"This is the victory that has overcome
the world, even our faith." (5:4)*

∾

We come now to the fourth piece of equipment in the
Christian soldier's armory—*the shield of faith*: "Above all," says
the apostle, "taking the shield of faith with which you will be
able to quench all the fiery darts of the wicked one" (Eph. 6:15,
NKJV).

Some take Paul's use of the expression "above all" to mean
"above everything else in importance," and from this they go on
to argue that the last three pieces of armor are more important
than the first three. But the phrase really means "in addition to
all this." It is a transition phrase designed to introduce us to a
section of the armor which has a different purpose.

The six pieces of armor fall clearly into two main groups, the
first consisting of the belt of truth, the breastplate of righteousness, and the shoes of the preparation of the gospel of
peace. The second group comprises the shield of faith, the
helmet of salvation, and the sword of the Spirit. The first three
pieces of armor were fixed to the body by a special fastening,

and hence, to a certain degree, were immovable. But the shield was not fixed to the body; it was something quite separate. The same applies to the helmet; that, too, was something that could be put on or taken off quite easily. And obviously the same was true of the sword of the Spirit.

The lesson, quite clearly, is this—the first three pieces of equipment should be worn at all times, while the other three are to be taken up when and where necessary.

PRAYER

Gracious and loving Heavenly Father, I am so thankful for the care and design that have gone into providing for me a sure defense against Satan. I have learned much, yet I see there is still much more to learn. Teach me, my Father. Amen.

∼

FURTHER STUDY

1 Tim. 1:12-20; 6:12; 1 Thess. 5:8
What had some rejected?
What was the result?

"HAVING" AND "TAKING"

FOR READING AND MEDITATION—
HEBREWS 11:1–16

"And without faith it is impossible to please God." (11:6)

~

We ended our last devotional thought by saying that the first three pieces of the Christian armor should be worn at all times, while the last three should be taken up and used when and where it is necessary. Evidence for this can be seen when we look at Paul's use of the words *having* and *taking.*

Listen again to the passage: "Stand therefore, having girded your waist with truth, having put on the breastplate of righteousness, and having shod your feet with the preparation of the gospel of peace" (NKJV). Then, in the second section, the word changes: "Above all, taking the shield of faith . . . take the helmet of salvation, and the sword of the Spirit" (NKJV). The difference between the first and last three pieces of equipment is the difference between "having" and "taking."

The "shield" referred to in Ephesians 6 was extremely large, about four feet long and about two and a half feet wide, designed to give as much protection as possible to the front of the body. More important, the front surface was covered with a sheet of fireproof metal so that the fiery darts of the enemy would have little or no effect. Clearly Paul thought that, in addition to the first three items, a further defense was needed to protect us from the devil's preliminary attacks.

When we consider the lengths to which God has gone in order to give us the protection we need against satanic attack, one wonders why we ever allow ourselves to be badgered and defeated by the devil.

PRAYER

O Father, once again I want to record my gratitude for the way in which You have provided for my defense against satanic attack. Help me to see, however, that it will do me no good just to appreciate it; I must use it. In Christ's name I will use it. Amen.

~

FURTHER STUDY

Heb. 11:17-40; Rom. 10:17; Phil. 3:8-9
How does faith come?
List some of the things accomplished through faith.

"FIERY DARTS"

*"The Lord stood at my side and gave me strength. . . .
And I was delivered from the lion's mouth." (4:17)*

～

The main purpose of the Roman shield was to protect soldiers from the fiery darts thrown at them by the enemy. These darts, made either of wood or metal, were covered with inflammable material and set alight immediately before being thrown. Enemies would throw these at each other in great numbers and from all directions so as to produce confusion. When thus attacked, a soldier would hold up the shield in front of him, allowing the fiery darts to land on the fireproof metal surface, from which they would drop away harmlessly.

The apostle says that we Christians need a "shield of faith"—in order "to quench all the fiery darts of the wicked" (KJV). An understanding of what these "fiery darts" are is essential if we are to stand firm against the adversary. Have you ever gone to bed at night feeling perfectly happy, only to wake in a sad mood? If there was no obvious physical or psychological reason for this, the chances are that you have experienced one of Satan's "fiery darts."

Sometimes they come as evil thoughts which intrude suddenly into our thinking, often at the most incongruous times. We may be reading the Bible, we may be praying, when all of a sudden some filthy thought flashes into our mind. It is a "fiery dart" from the devil. These do not come from inside us but from outside us. They strike us. Some thoughts do arise from within our carnal nature, but these of which I am speaking come from without—from Satan. And we are foolish if we do not recognize this and deal with them in this light.

PRAYER

O Father, help me to be alert and able to recognize the "fiery darts" of Satan when they are hurled at me. For I see that it is only when I recognize them that I can deal effectively with them. Give me insight and understanding. In Jesus' name. Amen.

FURTHER STUDY

James 1:1-22; 1 Cor. 10:13; 2 Cor. 11:3
What is the progression in temptation?
What was Paul's concern?

THE SATANIC STRATEGY

FOR READING AND MEDITATION—
JOHN 13:1–11

*"The devil had already put it into the heart of
Judas Iscariot . . . to betray him." (13:2, RSV)*

~

We are seeing that the "fiery darts" of the devil are quite different from the thoughts that are generated by our carnal nature. These "fiery darts" come *at* us rather than from *within* us. A satanic attack can usually be differentiated from something that arises within by the force with which the thought hits us. Thoughts that arise out of the carnal nature are offensive, but the thoughts that come as "fiery darts" from the devil burn.

Many Christians have told me that they often experience these attacks when they go to read their Bibles or to pray. When they read a newspaper, nothing seems to happen. But when they turn their attention to something spiritual, they find it almost impossible to concentrate, by reason of the shameful thoughts that occupy their minds.

The other thing one notices about these attacks is that they seem to come in cycles. They are not there permanently, but they come at certain times and seasons. I once counseled a man for one hour a week over a period of a whole year, and got him to write down in his diary the times and dates when he felt under satanic attack. When we looked through his diary together at the end of the year, we discovered an amazing thing—every single attack took place immediately prior to him doing something special for the Lord, like leading a Bible study, conducting a service, visiting the sick, or giving a public testimony. I shall never forget the expression on his face as he looked at me and said: "Who says that Satan isn't a strategist?"

PRAYER

My Father and my God, I realize that even though Satan is a strategist, he is no match for You. You know how to outmaneuver his every move. Help me to stay close to You, that I might experience Your strategy and not his. Amen.

~

FURTHER STUDY

Gen. 3; Matt. 4:1-10
How did Satan seek to penetrate Eve's mind?
How does this correlate with the temptation of Christ?

BLASPHEMOUS THOUGHTS

FOR READING AND MEDITATION—
2 CORINTHIANS 2:1–11

"For we are not unaware of his schemes." (2:11)

❧

Now we begin looking at a form of satanic attack which is probably the most difficult of all to endure. I refer to the matter of blasphemous thoughts. Dr. Martyn Lloyd-Jones said on this: "The devil has often plagued some of the noblest saints with blasphemous thoughts—blasphemous thoughts about God, blasphemous thoughts about the Lord Jesus Christ, and blasphemous thoughts about the Holy Spirit."

How horrible and terrifying such thoughts can be. Sometimes the devil hurls the most awful words and phrases into the mind; but again, it is important to see that these do not arise from within the heart of the believer—they come from the devil, who is trying to confuse and demoralize you.

How grateful we should be to the saints down the ages who have recorded these satanic attacks, for otherwise we would be tempted when experiencing them to believe that they have never happened to anyone else. Many masters of the spiritual life have described these satanic attacks in great detail—John Bunyan and Martin Luther being the two best examples.

But how do we deal with these "fiery darts" of Satan? What action must we take to repel these devilish attacks? There is only one answer—we must take and use the shield of faith. Faith alone enables us to meet and overcome this particular type of attack. What we must *not* do is expose our chests, expecting the breastplate of righteousness to deal with this problem. Each piece of the equipment is designed to deal with a particular attack. And the answer here is—faith.

PRAYER

Heavenly Father, I understand the problem—
now show me how to apply the answer. The answer, I see,
is faith. But how does it work? How can I apply it?
Teach me more. In Jesus' name. Amen.

~

FURTHER STUDY

2 Cor. 10:1-5; Matt. 22:37-38; Eph. 1:22-23; James 4:7-8
In what ways does Satan attack the mind?
What is the scriptural antidote?

PROMPT ACTION

FOR READING AND MEDITATION—
ROMANS 10:1–18

"Faith comes by hearing, and hearing by the word of God." (10:17, NKJV)

❧

Prayerfully, we ask ourselves this question: how does faith act as a protective shield? First of all, we must understand what faith is and how the word is being used here by Paul in Ephesians 6:16.

A little boy, when asked to give a definition of faith, said: "Faith is believing something you know isn't true." Well, that is precisely what faith is *not*! Faith is believing what you know *to be* true! But it is even more than that—it is *acting* on what you know to be true.

Some people see faith as something vague and mysterious, but faith is one of the Christian's most practical commodities. Take this verse, for example: "Faith without deeds is dead" (James 2:26). There is always the element of activity in faith; it prompts us to action. "Faith is the assurance of things hoped for, the conviction of things not seen" (Heb. 11:1, NASB).

Taking the shield of faith, then, is responding to the things the devil hurls at us by the quick application of what we believe about God and His Word, the Bible. When Satan sends his "fiery darts" in our direction, we can either stand and lament the fact that we are being attacked, or quickly raise the shield of faith and remind ourselves that the devil is a liar from the very beginning. We affirm that because we are redeemed by the blood of Christ, the devil has no legal or moral right to taunt us. But believing this is not enough; it must be acted on—and acted on quickly.

PRAYER

Father, I see that when Satan throws his "fiery darts" at me I must act, and act quickly. Help my faith to be so strong that it will not need a "jump start" to get it going. This I ask in Jesus' name. Amen.

∽

FURTHER STUDY

James 2:14-26; Heb. 11:1; 1 John 5:4
How are we justified?
Write out your definition of faith.

"I AM YOUR SHIELD"

FOR READING AND MEDITATION—
GENESIS 14:18–24 & 15:1–6

"Abram believed the LORD, and he credited it to him as righteousness." (15:6)

∾

It is no good saying you believe God is stronger than the devil if you do not act on that belief. Faith not only believes this but acts on it by quickly standing up to the devil, and saying something similar to what David said when he stood before Goliath: "You come to me with a sword, with a spear, and with a javelin. But I come to you in the name of the LORD of hosts" (I Sam. 17:45, NKJV). You must never forget that God is much more powerful than the devil. Hold on to that, and quickly raise your shield whenever you experience an attack of Satan's "fiery darts."

The passage which introduces this devotion focuses on an incident in Abraham's life which took place when he was exhausted after making a great stand. Doubtless, Satan would have attacked him with thoughts like: "What is the point of all this action of God on your behalf, and all these promises, when you do not have an heir to carry on your line? God doesn't seem to have as much power as it would appear."

Abraham was fearful at this point until the Lord came to him and gave him these glorious words: "Do not be afraid, Abram. I am your shield, your exceedingly great reward" (15:1, NKJV).

"I am your shield." Hold on to that great truth, my friend, and when under attack, quickly lift it up and remind the devil that you belong to One whose power is endless and eternal. His promises are ever sure. That is what it means to hold up the shield of faith.

PRAYER

O God, how grateful I am for the sureness and certainty of Your Word. Once again I feel it entering into the core of my being. Help me to put these truths into practice the very moment I come under satanic attack. In Jesus' name I pray. Amen.

∼

FURTHER STUDY

Prov. 30:1-5; Deut. 33:29; Pss. 33:20; 59:11; 84:9
Why was Israel blessed?
What was the psalmist's continual testimony?

THE HELMET OF SALVATION

FOR READING AND MEDITATION—
2 CORINTHIANS 11:1–15

*"I am afraid that just as Eve was deceived . . .
your minds may somehow be led astray." (11:3)*

~

The second piece of armor which is not tied or fixed to the
body but which a Christian soldier has to take up and put on
is "the helmet of salvation" (Eph. 6:17). The helmet worn by
a Roman soldier was usually made of bronze or iron with an
inside lining of felt or sponge. In some cases a hinged visor
added frontal protection. When a Roman soldier saw an enemy
coming, he would take hold of his shield, put on his helmet,
take his sword in hand, and stand alert and ready to do battle.

The figure of a helmet immediately suggests to us that this
is something designed to protect the mind, the intelligence, the
ability to think and reason. Just as the breastplate of righteousness protects us from *emotional* distress, the helmet of salvation
protects us from *mental* distress. This helmet can help us keep
our thinking straight and preserve us from mental confusion.

Has there ever been a time in history when we needed something to keep our thinking straight more than we do now?
Politicians vacillate and oscillate between despairing pessimism

and unrealistic optimism. Just think of the staggering complexities of the issues we face in our current generation—AIDS, violence, nuclear missiles, international tensions, economic instability, inner-city slums, and so on. The intelligentsia of our day confess to being utterly baffled in dealing with the problems with which human society is confronted. Where can we turn to ease the pressure on our minds? The only answer is God—in the helmet of salvation which He provides.

PRAYER

O Father, I am so grateful that You have provided freedom from that most terrifying of human problems—mental distress. Teach me all I need to know in applying Your truth to the important area of my mind. In Jesus' name. Amen.

≈

FURTHER STUDY

Eph. 4:1-17; Rom. 8:7; Col. 1:21
How were the Ephesians not to live?
How powerful is the influence of the mind?

THE TENSES OF SALVATION

"Let us be self-controlled, putting on faith and love as a breastplate, and the hope of salvation as a helmet." (5:8)

~

Satan will take advantage of every situation that comes his way in order to disable a Christian, and he will not hesitate to use chaotic world conditions and problems to oppose the mind. But God's answer to this is the helmet of salvation.

Paul is not talking here about the salvation of the soul. He is not referring to salvation as regeneration or conversion. This is the mistake that many make when attempting to interpret this verse. They say: "Whenever the devil attacks your mind and seeks to oppress it, remind yourself that you have been saved." Well, there is nothing wrong with that, of course. This explanation is mistaken, however, not because it is untrue, but because it does not go far enough.

The best way to interpret any verse of Scripture is with another verse of Scripture. Thus the text before us today throws a shaft of light on Paul's statement in Ephesians 6:17, for it shows salvation, not just as something in the past, but something that is also a future "hope." He uses the word *salvation* the same way in Romans when he writes: "Our salvation is nearer now than when we first believed" (Rom. 13:11).

In the Bible, the word *salvation* has three distinct tenses—past, present, and future. At conversion, we are saved from the *penalty* of sin. At present, day by day, we are being saved from the *power* of sin. And one day in the future, we will be saved from the *presence* of sin. It is to the future Paul is looking when he invites us to put on the helmet of salvation.

PRAYER

O Father, thank You for reminding me of the tenses of salvation. I see that in order to live effectively, I must view the present tense by the future tense. Help me lay hold on this. In Jesus' name. Amen.

∼

FURTHER STUDY

Pss. 27:1-14; 37:39; Isa. 12:2; 25:9
What was the psalmist's conviction?
What was the prophet proclaiming?

An Atheist's Lost "Faith"

"For in this hope we were saved." (8:24)

~

What is Paul talking about in this passage from Romans 8? He is talking about the time when Christ will return, when the kingdom of God will be established, and when creation will be delivered from bondage.

The helmet of salvation, therefore, is the recognition that all human schemes, all human disorder, and all human chaos will one day be ended. And when this happens, the whole universe will see that God has been quietly working out His purposes in and through everything.

This truth, when understood and embraced, is the one thing above all others that will enable us to keep our thinking straight in a world that is full of confusion and darkness. Why is it that thoughtful minds like H. G. Wells, Bernard Shaw, and others were and are so bewildered by what they see in the world? It is because they pin their hopes on unreliable and unrealistic resources. As the dean of Melbourne wrote about H. G. Wells: "He hailed science as a panacea for all ills and the goddess of knowledge and power."

But what were H. G. Wells's conclusions about the world before he died? He wrote this: "The science to which I pinned my faith is bankrupt. Its counsels, which should have established the millennium, led instead directly to the suicide of Europe. I believed them once. In their name I helped destroy the faith of millions of worshipers in the temples of a thousand creeds. And now they look at me and witness the great tragedy of an atheist who has lost his faith." There is no protection in the world for the mind.

PRAYER

Something, my Father, is being burned into my consciousness—there is just no hope outside of You. If I break with You, I break with sanity. Help me to walk closely with You so that Your mind becomes my mind. In Jesus' name. Amen.

~

FURTHER STUDY

Titus 2; Prov. 14:32; Acts 24:15; Col. 1:5
How should we live?
What are we to look for?

IT'S ALL UNDER CONTROL

FOR READING AND MEDITATION—
EPHESIANS 1:3–14

". . . according to His purpose who works all things after the counsel of His will." (1:11, NASB)

~

We are seeing that the salvation spoken of in the phrase, "the helmet of salvation," is the salvation we are going to enjoy when God works out His eternal purposes.

The Christian has a hope for the future. He has an understanding that God is working out His purposes in history, and therefore we need not be disturbed when human programs appear to be going wrong. We hear about "new deals" and "fair deals" and "better deals," yet they end up in disappointment for all concerned.

The Christian expects the world to get worse and worse, for this is what the Bible tells us will happen. He expects false teachings to abound. He expects the world's systems to fail, for anything that is not built on Christ has no guarantee of success. The Christian knows that wars and international tension are unavoidable, even though every effort is made to avoid them. The world is in such a state and such a condition that the more attention we give it, the more weary our minds become.

What is a Christian to do in such a world as ours? How are we to react when the devil takes advantage of our sensitivities to world conditions and focuses our thoughts upon them? Shall we give up? Shall we withdraw from life?

No, we put on the helmet of salvation and remind ourselves that in the face of everything that appears contrary, God is working out His eternal plan and purpose. History remains *His*-story! Almighty God is at work in the very events that appear to be filled with darkness and confusion.

PRAYER

O God, help me see that although You are apart from the events of history, You are also in the events of history. Ultimately all things are going to glorify You. Thank You, Father. Amen.

FURTHER STUDY

Heb. 6; 1 Pet. 1:3; 1 John 3:3
What does this hope provide for us?
How does Peter describe our hope?

"NOT A PRIVATE FIGHT"

*"Do not be afraid or discouraged . . .
For the battle is not yours, but God's." (20:15)*

❦

As I have been saying, the spiritual application of the helmet of salvation is not so much the enjoyment of our present salvation (though it includes that) as it is the assurance that a sure salvation is coming—and is even now at work.

This is what we need to know if we are to prevent the devil from bringing us into a state of mental distress—not merely that things will finally end right, but that God's plan is being worked out now. "History," writes Ray Stedman, an American Bible teacher, "is not a meaningless jumble but a controlled pattern, and the Lord Jesus Christ is the one who is directing these events."

The attack of Satan on the mind proceeds differently. He says to us: "Just look around you at the state of the world. God seems powerless to put things right. He has given lots of promises that things will one day get better, but none has come to pass. Hadn't you better give up this foolish idea that it's all going to work out right?"

If you were to let your mind dwell on that kind of satanic argument, you would soon find yourself in distress. The answer is to put on the helmet, the hope of salvation. You must remind yourself that things are not as they appear. The battle is not ours, but the Lord's. We may be individual soldiers fighting in the army of God, but the ultimate cause is sure and the end is certain. We need not be unduly troubled by what is happening in the world, for our commander is not just winning—He has already won!

PRAYER

Lord Jesus, I am grateful that the cross is the guarantee that neither sin nor Satan will ever defeat You. Your victory at Calvary has settled forever the question of who has the final word in the universe. I am so deeply, deeply thankful. Amen.

FURTHER STUDY

Luke 21:10-28; John 14:1-4; 16:33
How did Jesus describe the world?
What did He say to His disciples?

WE SEE JESUS

*"We do not see everything subject to him.
But we see Jesus."* (2:8-9)

~

Are you troubled as you look out at the situation in the world? Well, according to the Bible, things are going to get worse. As Jesus said: "Men's hearts failing them from fear and the expectation of those things which are coming on the earth" (Luke 21:26, NKJV). How are Christians going to stand when the darkness deepens and things get very much worse? What will we do when international tension increases?

Christians have a glorious hope—the hope of salvation. It is this, and this alone, which enables believers to live out their lives free from mental distress. I am sure you have already discovered that after reading the morning newspaper, you move into the day feeling somewhat depressed. Why is this? It is because almost daily, our newspapers are filled with murder, rape, violence, economic distress, child abuse. And our conscience, which through conversion has been sensitized to the moral laws of God, begins to reverberate as it comes up against the reports of things we know are contrary to the divine principles.

Satan, seeing our concern, attempts to exploit it to his own ends. "Things are getting worse, aren't they?" he says. "Why don't you just admit that God has lost control of His world?" If we did not have the helmet of salvation to put on at such a moment, we would finish up with the same attitude as H. G. Wells, who, after the Second World War, wrote: "The spectacle of evil in the world has come near to breaking my spirit." Again I say, there is no protection in the world for the mind.

PRAYER

My Father and my God, where would I be if I could not cling to a text such as that in my reading for today? My spirit too would be near to breaking. I am so thankful that in You there is hope—hope with a capital H.

∾

FURTHER STUDY

John 17; Rom. 8:35-37; 1 John 5:4
What did Jesus pray for His disciples?
What was Paul's conviction?

An Undisturbed Mind

For reading and meditation—
Colossians 1:9–28

". . . Christ in you, the hope of glory." (1:27)

∼

In the British Isles we are relatively free from much of what concerns and distresses others. We have much to be sad about, but we have much to be glad about also. We can still preach the gospel in our churches and can still enjoy freedom of speech. But I know that these pages will be read in areas of the world where this is not possible, where Satan is openly worshiped and where faith is not allowed to be expressed openly.

What do Christians living in these places do to prevent themselves from becoming wearied by their adverse circumstances? There is only one thing they can do—they must put on the helmet of the hope of salvation. This, more than anything, will help keep their thinking straight.

But no matter where in the world we live, those of us who have enlisted in the army of God must do the same. We must not succumb to the popular delusion that the working out of all human problems lies just around the corner through the application of humanistic ideas. Almost from the dawn of history, men and women have been grasping after the elusive hope that something can be worked out here. But God has never said this. Consistently throughout the Scriptures, He has said that fallen humanity is totally unable to work out its problems.

We know, however, that He has reserved a day of salvation when all wrongs will be righted, and it is only in the strength of the hope of that day of salvation that our hearts and minds can be kept undisturbed.

PRAYER

O Father, how can I ever be grateful enough that I am caught up in an eternal purpose. I live in the present, yet I draw also from the certainties of the future. Nourish this hope within me until it drives out every fear. In Jesus' name. Amen.

∽

FURTHER STUDY

Gal. 2; John 14:20; 1 John 3:24
How did Paul describe his Christian walk?
How would you describe your Christian walk?

THE SWORD OF THE SPIRIT

"Stand firm against the devil; resist him and he will flee from you." (4:7, AMPLIFIED)

❧

The last of the six pieces in the Christian's armor is "the sword of the Spirit, which is the word of God" (Eph. 6:17). John Stott points out that "of all the six pieces of armor or weaponry listed, the sword is the only one which can clearly be used for attack as well as defense." And the kind of attack envisaged here is one that involves a close encounter, for the word used for sword is *machaira*, meaning a short sword or dagger.

There is much more to spiritual warfare than standing up to the devil. We possess, according to the above text, the potential to make him "flee." The word *flee* is a very strong word in the original Greek. It means much more than just a strategic withdrawal; it means beating a swift retreat. What an amazing truth! It is possible for a Christian so to resist the devil that he races away as fast as he can.

This truth must not be seen in any way as limiting the devil's power, for he is a strong and determined foe. It means rather that a Christian able to wield the sword of the Spirit can ensure that Satan is overpowered. We are right to develop a healthy respect for the devil's wiles, but we are wrong when we allow him to terrorize us.

We must have the assurance, given everywhere in the New Testament, that to engage in conflict with the devil is not a hopeless task. We are not to indulge in overconfidence but, at the same time, we are not to be frightened by him.

PRAYER

*O Father, the thought that I, a sinner saved by grace,
am able to send Satan into retreat almost overwhelms me.
Yet I must believe it, for Your Word tells me so. Help me
understand even more clearly the authority I have
in Christ. In His name I ask it. Amen.*

~

FURTHER STUDY

Luke 10:1-20; Acts 3:6-8; 16:16-18; 1 Pet. 5:8-9
How much authority over Satan have we been given?
How did the early church exercise this authority?

PRECISE SCRIPTURE

FOR READING AND MEDITATION—
MATTHEW 4:1–11

"It is written . . . It is also written . . ."
(4:4, 7)

∼

We must now focus on what is meant by the phrase—"the sword of the Spirit, which is the word of God." The sword is the Word of God—the Bible, the inspired Scriptures.

In the passage before us at present, we see a perfect illustration of how Jesus used the sword of the Spirit when rebutting the temptations of the devil. Notice how, prior to the temptation, Jesus was anointed by the Holy Spirit (Matt. 3:13–17). Next we are informed that Jesus was "led by the Spirit into the desert to be tempted by the devil" (4:1).

During the temptation our Lord, filled with the Spirit, resisted every one of the devil's statements by using the precise words of Scripture. Follow me closely, for this is extremely important: Christ did not merely utter a newly formed statement or something that came to Him on the spur of the moment, but quoted a text which had already been given by God and written down. The weapon used by our Lord was the Word of God, the Scriptures.

Can you see the point I am making? Satan is not rebuffed by clever phrases that are made up on the spur of the moment and sound theologically sophisticated and refined. He is defeated only when we quote to him the precise words of Scripture. If this was the strategy Jesus had to use, then how much more you and I.

Nothing defeats Satan more thoroughly and effectively than the sword of the Spirit, which is the Word of God.

PRAYER

O God, open my eyes that I might see more clearly than ever the power and authority that lies in Your sacred Word, the Bible. Help me to know it better. For Your own dear name's sake. Amen.

∾

FURTHER STUDY

1 Pet. 1:13-25; Ps. 119:89, 103; Jer. 15:16
What did Jeremiah do with God's word?
How did the psalmist describe it?

AN INSPIRED BOOK

FOR READING AND MEDITATION—
JOHN 16:1–15

*"When he, the Spirit of truth, comes,
he will guide you into all truth." (16:13)*

～

Why are the Scriptures described as a sword provided by the Holy Spirit? Quite simply, it is the Holy Spirit who has given us the Scriptures. They come altogether from Him.

It was the Holy Spirit who inspired men to write them: "Men spoke from God as they were carried along by the Holy Spirit" (2 Pet. 1:21). Again in 2 Timothy 3:16 we read: "All Scripture is God-breathed"—a statement which assures us that the Scriptures come from the Holy Spirit.

The Bible is not a mere human document. The Holy Spirit breathed into men and inspired them to write the way they did. This does not mean that the people who wrote the Scriptures did so mechanically, in the way that someone would dictate into a dictating machine. The Holy Spirit used their natural way of expression, but gave them an additional ability to write without error.

It is vital, if you are to win the battle against Satan, that you not only see this truth but believe it. When you consider how

powerful Satan is, you need something that is even more powerful. The Bible, the inspired Word of God, is your strength.

One step further—only the Holy Spirit can enable us truly
to understand God's Word: "We have not received the spirit of
the world but the Spirit who is from God, that we may understand what God has freely given us" (1 Cor. 2:12). Without the
Holy Spirit, we would be no more able to understand the
Scriptures than a blind man could judge a beauty contest.

PRAYER

*Gracious Holy Spirit, just as You breathed into the
Bible to give it its life and power, breathe also into my heart
today so that I might know and understand its truth.
I ask this in Jesus' name. Amen.*

FURTHER STUDY

Col. 3:1-16; Deut. 6:6; 11:18; Heb. 10:15-16
What does the word "dwell" mean?
Where must God's word be written?

"DIVIDE AND CONQUER"

*"The things that come from the Spirit of God
. . . are spiritually discerned." (2:14)*

～

Only the Holy Spirit can help us properly to interpret the Word of God. A person may have a fine mind, a good seminary training, even a theological degree, but none of these is a sufficient foundation on which to attempt to interpret the Word of God. Truth, as the above text tells us, is "spiritually discerned."

But there is one more thing we need to understand—only the Holy Spirit can show us how to use it aright. Doubtless, this was the consideration in the mind of the apostle when he penned the statement we are considering: "the sword of the Spirit, which is the word of God." It is one thing to know the *contents* of Scripture; it is another thing to know how to *use* those contents in a way that defeats the devil. Only the Holy Spirit can enable us to do this.

The relationship between the Holy Spirit and the Word of God is an important one. Some tend to put the emphasis on one side or the other. But the moment we separate the Spirit and the Word, we are in trouble. The late Donald Gee once said: "All Spirit and no Word, you blow up. All Word and no Spirit, you dry up. Word and Spirit—you grow up."

Without the Spirit, the Word is a dead letter; with the Spirit, it is a living and powerful force. The devil has a policy of "divide and conquer." And if he can get us to separate the Word from the Spirit, then he has us just where he wants us.

PRAYER

My Father, I see that when I separate the Spirit from the Word and the Word from the Spirit, I am in trouble. Help me to be as open to the Spirit as I am to the Bible, and as open to the Bible as I am to the Spirit. In Jesus' name. Amen.

FURTHER STUDY

2 Cor. 3:1-6; John 6:63; 1 Pet. 3:18
What "gives life"?
What made Paul an able minister of truth?

THE DIVINE DESIGN

"The Holy Spirit . . . will teach you all things and will remind you of everything I have said to you." (14:26)

～

When we come to God's Word, laying aside all preconceived ideas and depending entirely on the Holy Spirit to reveal its truth to us, we put ourselves in a position where the Holy Spirit can impress the truth of the Scriptures into our innermost being. There it takes root within us, and whenever we stand in need of a word with which to rebut the devil, the Holy Spirit brings it to our remembrance.

And here's the most wonderful thing—the Word of God on our lips will have the same effect upon the devil as if he were hearing it from the lips of Jesus Himself! Every time we open the Bible, we must be careful to pray for the illumination of the Spirit so that we don't finish up making the Bible say what we want it to say. When we receive that help, we are following the divine design—letting the Spirit bring home to our hearts the truth and meaning of His own Word.

This attitude of humility and receptivity gives the Holy Spirit the opportunity He needs to build the truth of the Word of God into our spirits. Approaching the Bible in this way, said the late J. B. Phillips, "is like rewiring a house where the electricity has not been turned off." As we read the Scriptures, we are touching something that has a current of power flowing through its pages—a power not put there by any man. The Holy Spirit has gone into it, so is it any wonder that the Holy Spirit comes out of it?

PRAYER

My Father and my God, I know the Spirit dwells in Your Word. I come to ask that He might dwell also in me, to open up my whole being to the truth and power that lies in its inspired pages. In Jesus' name I ask it. Amen.

~

FURTHER STUDY

John 15:18-27; Luke 12:11-12; Rom. 8:14
What did Jesus declare about the Holy Spirit's ministry?
What promise did Jesus give to His disciples?

THE COAL MINER

*"For the word of God is living and active.
Sharper than any double-edged sword . . ." (4:12)*

~

Some of you reading these lines today may not have had the benefits of a good or extensive education. You may be deficient in your knowledge of many things. But here is the encouraging thing—none of these issues are important when it comes to the matter of defeating Satan.

I remember being present some years ago in a church in South Wales when a debate was held between a university professor and an ordinary coal miner. The subject was: "Is the Bible true?" The university professor presented his arguments in a clear fashion, and I remember feeling quite sorry for the miner as I envisaged some of the difficulties he might face when making his reply. After the professor had finished, the miner stood to his feet. And for over an hour, I witnessed one of the most amazing demonstrations of the Holy Spirit at work that I have ever seen in my life.

The miner began by asking everyone to bow their heads as he prayed a prayer which went something like this: "Lord, I have not had much education, but You know that I love Your Word and have spent my life searching its pages. Help me now to say something that will convince my friends here that Your Word is true." He then proceeded to demolish the arguments of the professor simply by quoting appropriate Scriptures without making even a simple comment.

When he finished, there was thunderous applause. The professor's well-articulated, highly intellectual arguments had been torn to pieces by the sharp edges of the sword of the Spirit— by that and by that alone.

PRAYER

O Father, the more I hear, the more I want to hear.
For I was created by Your Word, designed according to Your
Word, and I can never remain content until I am indwelt with
Your Word. Teach me even more. In Jesus' name. Amen.

FURTHER STUDY

Jer. 5:1-14; 23-29; Ps. 119:105, 130
What was God's word in Jeremiah's mouth?
What was it to the psalmist?

GO STILL DEEPER

"Your word is truth." (17:17)

~

Christians who do not accept the authority of the Scriptures have no effective weapon with which to overcome Satan. It is as simple as that. If you are not certain that the Bible is the Word of God, if you do not believe that it is without error in all that it affirms, then you are like a soldier with a broken sword.

To use the sword of the Spirit effectively, we need to have as wide a knowledge of the Bible as possible. Let me take you back once again to Christ's encounter with Satan in the wilderness of temptation. When Satan advanced, Jesus took up the sword of the Spirit and knew exactly which particular Scriptures to use to rebut each of the three separate temptations of the devil.

If we are to conquer Satan in the same way that Jesus conquered him, then we must know the Bible in its entirety. It is no good saying to the devil: "The verse I want to use against you is somewhere in the Bible." You must quote it to him and quote it precisely.

I hope you do not think that reading this little book of mine will do this for you, because it won't. These devotional readings will help you start the day, but you need a deeper and more intensive program of study if you are to become proficient in the use of the Scriptures against Satan. Decide right now to commit yourself to exploring the Bible more deeply and thoroughly than you have ever done before.

PRAYER

O Father, I see that the more I know of Your Word,
the more effective I will be in resisting Satan. Show me
how to go more deeply into the Scriptures than I have
ever done before. In Jesus' name I pray. Amen.

FURTHER STUDY

Ezek. 37:1-10; Acts 17:11; Rom. 10:8
What was the result of the spoken word through Ezekiel?
What did Paul say of the Bereans?

A FINAL EXHORTATION

FOR READING AND MEDITATION—
LUKE 21:20–36

"Be always on the watch, and pray." *(21:36)*

〜

One might think that, having examined in detail the six pieces of the armor of God, this would be a natural place to end our discussion, but there is one more verse to consider: "Praying always with all prayer and supplication in the Spirit, being watchful to this end with all perseverance and supplication for all the saints" (Eph. 6:18, NKJV).

What is the meaning of this further and final exhortation? Well, it is not, as so many Christians believe, an additional but unnamed piece of armor. One commentator writes: "Paul is giving us in this verse the final piece of armor for the Christian who is in conflict with the devil: praying always with all prayer. . . ." This surely cannot be so, for Paul's reference to "praying always with all prayer"—although closely related to the six pieces of armor—is quite different from them and does not fall within the bounds of the careful and close analogy that he has been making.

What then does he mean? He is saying (so I believe) that "praying in the Spirit" is something that ought to pervade all our spiritual warfare, and is something we have to do—and *keep on doing*—if we are to win the battle against Satan and his forces. Paul is saying: "Put on the whole armor of God, every single piece, and in the proper order; but in addition to that, at all times and in all places, keep on praying." In other words, the armor which is provided for us by God cannot be used effectively unless it is worn by a praying Christian.

PRAYER

*O Father, thank You for inspiring Your servant Paul
to give us this insight, for we see that without it we would
be defeated by the devil. Help me become a watchful and
praying Christian. In Jesus' name. Amen.*

FURTHER STUDY

Luke 18:1-8; 1 Chron. 16:11; Col. 4:2; 1 Thess. 5:17
What was Jesus teaching in this parable?
How did Paul exhort the Colossians?

NOT A POSTSCRIPT

*"We always thank God, the Father of our Lord
Jesus Christ, when we pray for you." (1:3)*

~

We saw in the previous reading that we must not think, when
Paul finishes his description of the Christian's armor in
Ephesians 6:17, that he has ended his exhortation. In fact, if we
were to stop there, we would miss the whole meaning of the
apostle's thought, for the six pieces of armor only provide us
with adequate defense against the devil when they are worn by
a praying Christian.

Ephesians 6:18, therefore, is not a postscript but more of a
culmination of all that the apostle has been saying before.
"Stand praying," cries the great apostle, "always with all prayer
and supplication in the Spirit."

The danger facing us is that we can feel, once we have our
spiritual armor on, that we are safe, thinking all is well, that the
armor will protect us. But this is the height of folly and something Satan would love to get us to believe. If we do believe it,
then it means we are already defeated. The armor of God and
its spiritual application must always be thought of in terms of

our relationship with God. If there is no communion with Him, then the six pieces of armor will be ineffective. The armor of God is not something that is magical or mechanical; it functions as a spiritual defense only when worn with prayer. One of the great hymns of our faith expresses the thought:

To keep your armor bright
Attend with constant care
Still walking in our Captain's sight
And watching unto prayer.

PRAYER

Father, I see that with all I have learned about defending myself against the devil, I must still go a step further. Help me to understand this step, for it is vital that I am not just protected against Satan, but fully protected. Amen.

∼

FURTHER STUDY

John 15:1-7; Jer. 29:13; Matt. 26:41; Mark 11:24
Why can we pray with confidence?
What must accompany prayer?

And Yet . . .

"Be unceasing in prayer—praying perseveringly."
(5:17, AMPLIFIED)

❧

John Stott, in his commentary on Ephesians, says: "Equipping ourselves with God's armor is not a mechanical operation; it is in itself an expression of our dependence upon God."

Note the phrase, "is not a mechanical operation." Some Christians like to begin each day by going through the motions of dressing themselves in the armor of God. In their minds they put on the belt of truth, the breastplate of righteousness, the shoes of the preparation of the gospel of peace, and so on. I have no objection to this myself, but I do see a danger that it can become merely a mechanical operation in which they look just to the armor to protect them from the wiles of the devil, thinking that nothing more needs to be done.

Let me remind you again—every single piece of armor, excellent and valuable though it is in itself, will not work for us unless always, and at all times, we are in a close, prayerful relationship with God.

Cast your mind back once again over the six pieces of the Christian soldier's equipment: the belt of truth, the breastplate of righteousness, the shoes of peace, the shield of faith, the helmet of salvation, and the sword of the Spirit. What strong protection our Lord has provided for us in this conflict against Satan and his forces! And yet, having all this great and wonderful equipment, we can still suffer defeat if we do not stand in the strength and power which God provides. And that power can flow only along the channel of fervent, believing prayer.

PRAYER

Father, day by day it is becoming increasingly clear that unless I am continually linked to Your resources through believing prayer, the armor You have provided for me gives me only a limited defense. Help me never to forget this. Amen.

FURTHER STUDY

Col. 1:1-12; Phil. 4:13; Eph. 3:16; 1 Pet. 5:10
What was Paul's prayer for the Colossians?
Where does our strength come from?

Standard Procedure

*"I want men everywhere to lift up holy hands
in prayer, without anger or disputing."* (2:8)

~

We are considering the fact that we can meticulously put on every piece of God's armor and yet suffer defeat by the devil if we do not go on to consider the injunction—"praying always with all prayer." Dr. Martyn Lloyd-Jones says: "I have known Christians who have been well acquainted with the theology of the Bible and known it in an extraordinary manner, but who did not believe in prayer meetings, who did not seem to see the utter and absolute necessity of 'praying always' in the way that is indicated here by the apostle."

It is possible to be orthodox in your doctrine and still, as far as spiritual warfare is concerned, be a defeated Christian. You cannot fight the devil, even with orthodoxy, if you know nothing of a vital, day-by-day relationship with God through prayer. Many people have a wonderful understanding of Scripture and are experts at pointing out the errors in other people's teaching, but because they do not have a close relationship with God in prayer, they fall easy prey to the devil.

Even a whole church or community of Christian people can experience this same problem. They can have a good, sound knowledge of the Bible, yet know nothing of a strong corporate ministry of prayer. Such a church can be easily paralyzed by the devil. It may seem that I am laboring the point, but it is absolutely imperative for us to understand that our effectiveness in spiritual warfare depends not on the armor alone, but on our ability to maintain a close and intimate relationship with God through prayer.

PRAYER

Father, I think I have it now—without prayer, everything else fails to work the way You designed it to. Drive this truth so deeply into my spirit that for the rest of my life, it will be my standard operating procedure. Amen.

∼

FURTHER STUDY

Luke 11:1-13; 6:12; Mark 1:35; 6:46-47
What was the disciples' request?
What was Jesus' pattern?

THE FOUR "ALLS"

FOR READING AND MEDITATION—
MATTHEW 14:22–33

*"He went up on a mountainside
by himself to pray." (14:23)*

~

If, as we have seen, the effectiveness of our spiritual warfare depends not just on wearing the six pieces of armor, but also on constant, believing prayer, then we must ask ourselves: what can we do to make our prayer lives more contributive?

The place given to prayer in both the Old and New Testaments is remarkable. All the great saints of the Old Testament knew how to pray—Abraham, David, Daniel, Jeremiah, Isaiah, to mention just a few. The same prowess in prayer can be seen also in the New Testament saints.

But of course the greatest Person of prayer was none other than our Lord Jesus Christ. Although He possessed great knowledge and wisdom, He found it essential to turn aside time and time again to pray. On certain occasions He would spend whole nights in prayer or rise long before dawn in order to pray and maintain His communion with God.

Is it surprising, therefore, that being so dependent on prayer, He should have told His disciples: "Men ought always to pray, and not to faint" (Luke 18:1, KJV). Praying is the only alternative to fainting—we must pray or else we faint.

Paul's teaching with regard to prayer in Ephesians 6:18 revolves around four "alls." We are to pray at *all* times, with *all* prayer, with *all* perseverance, and for *all* the saints. Most Christians, however, pray at *some* times, with *some* prayer, and *some* degree of perseverance for *some* of God's saints.

When we replace "some" by "all" in these expressions, we are on our way to effective praying.

PRAYER

My Father and my God, I see that through prayer,
You offer me the most breathtaking power. Help me humbly to
take it and use it wisely. In Jesus' name I pray. Amen.

❧

FURTHER STUDY

1 Sam. 7:1-10; 1:27; Exod. 15:24-25; 1 Kings 18:37-38
List some prayers God answered.
List some answers to prayer you have received.

VARIOUS FORMS OF PRAYER

*"Devote yourselves to prayer,
being watchful and thankful." (4:2)*

~

Today we ask ourselves: what does it mean to "pray always with all prayer and supplication"? The phrase "praying always" presents no difficulty; quite clearly, this means praying as often as possible, regularly and constantly. But what does it mean to pray "with all prayer and supplication"? Paul means, I believe, that we should pray with all forms or kinds of prayer.

You see, there are many different forms of prayer that are available to us. First, there is *verbal prayer* when we present our prayer to God in carefully chosen words and phrases. Second, there is *silent prayer*, when no words cross our lips, but prayer flows directly from our hearts. Third, there is *ejaculatory prayer*, when we express sounds rather than words, as when we sigh or groan in prayer. Then there is *public prayer*, common prayer, or "praying together"—or, as some prefer to call it, "praying in concert." So praying with "all prayer" means using every form of prayer available to us, praying in every way and manner we can. We are to be at it always, and in endless ways.

But there is a certain form of prayer to which the apostle refers which deserves our closer examination—the prayer of "supplication" or "petition"—when we pray with regard to special requests and needs. We must not overlook this, for it is so easy to be caught up in adoration and praise that we neglect to focus our prayers on the various needs that arise from time to time, not only in our own lives, but also in the lives of others. This, too, is a necessary kind of prayer.

PRAYER

Father, help me to see the senselessness of trying to muddle through life in my own strength when You have made Your power and resources available to me through prayer. Help me grow in prayer. In Jesus' name. Amen.

FURTHER STUDY

Matt. 7:1-12; Acts 1:14; 4:24; 12:12; 21:5
What is evident about the early church?
How does Jesus relate fatherhood to prayer?

"PRAYING IN THE SPIRIT"

FOR READING AND MEDITATION—
ROMANS 8:18–30

*"We do not know what we ought to pray for,
but the Spirit himself intercedes for us."* (8:26)

～

What does it mean to pray "in the Spirit"? Here again, there is a good deal of misunderstanding among Christians as to the true meaning of this phrase.

There are times when one feels deeply affected emotionally as one prays, but this is not the meaning of the phrase "praying in the Spirit." It has no relationship to the emotions that we feel in prayer. I am not saying that feelings are unimportant in prayer; I am simply saying that I do not believe this is what Paul had in mind when he used the phrase "praying in the Spirit."

The "spirit" spoken of here is not the human spirit but the Holy Spirit. Some believe that "praying in the Spirit" takes place when we pray in other tongues, and although it can include that, I believe it is much more than that.

Prayer that is "in the Spirit" is prayer that is prompted and guided by the Spirit. One commentator puts it this way: "It means that the Holy Spirit directs the prayer, creates the prayer within us, and empowers us to offer it and to pray it."

Dr. Martyn Lloyd-Jones calls praying in the Spirit "the secret of true prayer" and goes on to say: "If we do not pray in the Spirit, we do not really pray." I would hesitate to make such a sweeping statement myself, but I would go so far as to say that if we do not know what it means to pray in the Spirit, our prayers will have little impact upon Satan and his forces.

PRAYER

Dear Father, I have so much to learn about prayer that unless You take my hand and guide me, I can soon lose my way. Teach me how to enter the deeper levels of prayer. In Jesus' name. Amen.

FURTHER STUDY

Rom. 8:1-17; Luke 11:13; 24:49
To what does the Spirit bear witness?
What was Christ's promise to His disciples?

SPIRIT-AIDED PRAYING

"The Spirit gives life." (6:63)

∿

The more I consider "praying in the Spirit," the more con-
vinced I am that the majority of Christians do not know what
it means to pray in this particular way. Many are content to
recite prayers and know nothing of the thrill of entering a
dimension of prayer in which the Holy Spirit has full control.

Not that there is anything wrong with liturgical or written
prayers—they can be a wonderful primer for one's spiritual
pump. Many people tell me that the prayers I frame at the end
of each devotion in *Every Day with Jesus* have sometimes helped
them more than the actual notes I have written. Using written
prayers can be helpful, but we must heed the apostle's exhortation to move on into that dimension which he calls "praying in
the Spirit." The best description of this I have ever heard is
that given by some of the old Welsh preachers, like Daniel
Rowlands, Christmas Evans, and others. They describe it as
"praying with unusual liberty and freedom."

There is hardly anything more wonderful in the Christian life
than to experience this "liberty and freedom" in prayer. I can

remember the minister and elders of the church in which I was converted in South Wales saying after a prayer meeting in which there had been great liberty and power: "Tonight we have prayed in the Spirit."

Have you not experienced moments when, after struggling and halting in prayer, you were suddenly taken out of yourself and words just poured out of you? At that moment, you were "praying in the Spirit."

PRAYER

O Father, forgive me that I try to do so much in my own strength instead of learning how to let You do it in me. Teach me how to let go and let You take over in everything— particularly my praying. In Jesus' name. Amen.

≈

FURTHER STUDY

2 Cor. 3:6-18; Matt. 6:7-8; 1 Cor. 14:15; Jude 20
What does the Spirit of the Lord bring?
What are we to avoid when we pray?

FIRST PRINCIPLES

"Put out into deep water." (5:4)

❧

I find myself compelled to spend another day discussing Paul's pregnant phrase: "praying in the Spirit."

There are times in my own life, as I am sure there are in yours, when I struggle in prayer and find it difficult to concentrate, only to discover that suddenly I am taken out of myself and given a freedom that transforms my prayer time from that point on. When this happens, I know I have been praying in the Spirit. This is the kind of thing about which the apostle Paul is exhorting us in Ephesians 6:18. Formal prayer is fine and has its place, but oh, how we need to experience more times of praying in the Spirit.

But how do we attain these times? Is it the Spirit's responsibility to bring us there, or do we have some responsibility in the matter, too? I believe we can learn to pray in the Spirit.

Some first principles are these: (1) *Come to God in an attitude of dependence.* This means recognizing that your greatest need in prayer is not an ability to put words together or form fine phrases, but the Holy Spirit's empowerment. (2) *Yield yourself totally to the Spirit,* letting Him guide and direct your praying. Be continually aware that He wants to have the bigger part in your prayer life. Start with these two principles, learning to depend less and less on your own experience or ability and more and more on the Spirit's enabling. Once you experience what it means to "pray in the Spirit," you will long to experience it more and more.

PRAYER

O Father, my appetite is being whetted. Help me "launch out into the deep" and give myself to You in the way that You are willing to give Yourself to me. In Christ's name I ask it. Amen.

～

FURTHER STUDY

John 3:22-27; 2 Chron. 20:12; 2 Cor. 3:3-5
What was John's declaration?
How did Paul express his dependence on God?

NOT SOME . . . BUT ALL

FOR READING AND MEDITATION—
EPHESIANS 4:17–32

"For we are all members of one body." (4:25)

❧

We have two more phrases to consider before we bring to a close our meditations on Ephesians 6:10-20: (1) "Keep alert with all perseverance" and (2) "making supplication for all the saints" (Eph. 6:18, RSV).

The first phrase draws our attention to the fact that we should never allow ourselves to become indolent and lethargic in relation to this matter of prayer, but always eager and ready to make our requests known to Him. But what is the purpose of this spiritual watchfulness? This question brings us to the second phrase: "making supplication for all the saints." Our watchfulness and concern must not be only on our own behalf but on behalf of all other Christians also.

Why does Paul exhort us to pray for *all* rather than *some* Christians—those, for example, whom we know are enduring a particular attack of Satan? The answer is because all Christians need praying for! Every believer is under attack; no one is exempted from this condition. The letter of Jude tells us that we are partakers of a "common salvation." But not only do we enjoy a common salvation; we are fighting a common enemy. And in this we experience common difficulties—hence the need to be intensely aware of each other's needs. We cannot, of course, take the armor of God and put it on another Christian, but we can pray for one another and thus call in spiritual reinforcements. We can pray that their eyes might be opened to the danger they are in and that they might be able to equip themselves to stand against Satan and his powerful forces.

PRAYER

O Father, forgive me, I pray, that sometimes I am so taken up with my own spiritual struggles that I forget my brothers and sisters, who face the same difficulties also. Save me from my self-centeredness, dear Lord. In Jesus' name I pray. Amen.

FURTHER STUDY

Gen. 18:23-33; Matt. 15:21-28; Acts 12:5
How did Abraham intercede?
How did the Syrophoenician woman demonstrate persistence?

SATAN'S PINCER MOVEMENT

FOR READING AND MEDITATION—
LUKE 22:24–34

*"I have prayed for you, Simon,
that your faith may not fail."* (22:32)

∿

Another reason why the apostle Paul bids us pray for one another is this: the failure of any one of us is going to have some effect upon the spiritual campaign which God is waging against the devil through the church.

As we said on the first day of our meditations: all those who have committed themselves to Jesus Christ should know that the forces of two kingdoms—the kingdoms of God and of the devil—are locked together in mortal combat. And Christians, whether they like it or not, are thrust right onto the cutting edge of this conflict.

The battle line between the forces of God and the forces of Satan is the church—and that means you and me. What is Satan's best tactic in attempting to bring about the church's spiritual defeat? He probes at every point he can, looking for the weakest part. When he finds a weak Christian (or a group of weak Christians), he calls for reinforcements. Then, using what military strategists call "a pincer movement," he attempts to break through at that point. And when one Christian fails, all of us to some extent are affected, for we are all part of the one line of defense.

How the devil rejoices when an individual Christian falls—especially a church leader. Therefore, we are called to a ministry of prayer—not just for ourselves but for one another also—that we might stand perfect and complete in the will of God, and that our faith will not fail when under attack by the devil.

PRAYER

Father, I am encouraged as I think that today,
millions of Christians around the world will be praying
for me. Help me never to fail in my responsibility to pray
for them. In Christ's peerless and precious name. Amen.

FURTHER STUDY

Gal. 6:1-10; 1 Cor. 9:27; Phil. 3:12; James 5:16
What are we to carry in prayer?
Of what was Paul conscious?

PRAY FOR ME THAT . . .

FOR READING AND MEDITATION—
ROMANS 12:1–13

*"Be transformed by the renewing of your mind.
Then you will be able to . . . approve . . .
God's . . . perfect will." (12:2)*

～

The apostle ends this section on spiritual warfare (Eph. 6:10-20) on the following personal note: "Pray on my behalf, that utterance may be given to me in the opening of my mouth, to make known with boldness the mystery of the gospel . . . that in proclaiming it I may speak boldly, as I ought to speak" (vv. 19-20, NASB).

Paul was wise enough to know his own need of supernatural strength in being able to stand against the enemy, and he was humble enough to ask his brothers and sisters to pray for him in this matter.

Imagine this great apostle, probably the most powerful and effective disciple of Christ the world has ever seen, asking his friends to pray for him. Truly, the greater a Christian is, the more he realizes his dependence on the prayers of others. Paul knew full well the power that was against him, and he did not hesitate to ask for the prayers of the church in Ephesus.

Notice also that his request for prayer was clear and specific. When you ask someone to pray for you, be equally specific. Don't just say, "Pray for me," but "Pray for me that . . ." Paul's request was not that he might be delivered from prison, but that through his testimony in prison the gospel of Christ might be advanced. He knew that the most important thing was not to triumph *over* prison but to triumph *in* it. He knew he was where God wanted him for that time, and he would allow no self-interest to interfere with the divine schedule.

PRAYER

O Father, teach me, as You taught Your servant Paul,
to know Your will and purpose so clearly that I might
know just how and what to pray for. I ask this in and
through the strong and mighty name of Jesus. Amen.

∾

FURTHER STUDY

2 Thess. 3; 1 Thess. 5:25; Heb. 13:18-19
What was Paul's request?
Whom are you praying for regularly?

THE FINAL WORD

FOR READING AND MEDITATION—
EPHESIANS 3:8–21

*"Now, through the church, the manifold
wisdom of God should be made known to the . . .
authorities in the heavenly realms." (3:10)*

～

In this last devotional reading of our study on "The Armor
of God," we gather up what we have been saying on this important theme. Once we become Christians, we are involved in a
fight against Satan and his forces. God, however, has given us a
defense against Satan and his wiles, which consist of six separate pieces of spiritual equipment.

First, he has given us the *belt of truth*—a willingness to let
God's truth govern every part of our lives. Second, the *breastplate of righteousness*—seeing clearly that we are not saved by our
own righteousness but Christ's. Third, we must have our feet
shod with the preparation of the *gospel of peace*—our determi-
nation to stand firmly in the faith.

Fourth, we must raise the *shield of faith*—the quick action by
which we act upon God's truth and refuse Satan's lies. Fifth, we
must put on the *helmet of salvation*—the glorious hope that, one
day, the Lord will right all wrongs and establish His eternal

kingdom. And sixth, we must take up the *sword of the Spirit*, the Word of God, and wield the written Scriptures in the same way our Lord did in His wilderness temptations.

Yet we noted also that having done all this, it is still possible to be defeated by the devil unless we know how to pray in the power of the Spirit. We must pray not only when things are going wrong but continuously, fervently, powerfully, and perseveringly. Our prayers must catch alight and burst into flame. Against such praying, the principalities and powers are helpless.

PRAYER

My Father, now that I have seen the resources that are available to me in Christ, I realize that my responsibility to avail myself of these resources is greater than ever. Help me to put everything I have learned into action. For Your own dear name's sake. Amen.

∿

FURTHER STUDY

Pss. 18:1-50; 65:6; Hab. 3:19; Isa. 41:10
With what was David armed?
Have you put on your armor today?

OTHER BOOKS IN THIS SERIES

If you've enjoyed your experience with this devotional book, look for more Every Day with Jesus® titles by Selwyn Hughes.

Every Day with Jesus: The Lord's Prayer
0-8054-2735-X

Every Day with Jesus: The Spirit-Filled Life
0-8054-2736-8

Every Day with Jesus: The Character of God
0-8054-2737-6

Every Day with Jesus: Hinds' Feet, High Places
0-8054-3088-1

Every Day with Jesus: The Armor of God
0-8054-3079-2

Every Day with Jesus: Staying Spiritually Fresh
0-8054-3080-6

ALSO BY SELWYN HUGHES

Every Day Light   0-8054-0188-1
with paintings by Thomas Kinkade

Every Day Light: Water for the Soul   0-8054-1774-5
with paintings by Thomas Kinkade

Every Day Light: Light for the Path   0-8054-2143-2
with paintings by Larry Dyke

Every Day Light: Treasure for the Heart   0-8054-2428-8
with paintings by Larry Dyke

Every Day Light Devotional Journal   0-8054-3309-0

Christ Empowered Living   0-8054-2450-4

Cover to Cover   0-8054-2144-0
A Chronological Plan to Read the Bible in One Year

Hope Eternal   0-8054-1767-2

Jesus-The Light of the World   0-8054-2089-4
with paintings by Larry Dyke

The Selwyn Hughes Signature Series
Born to Praise   0-8054-2091-6
Discovering Life's Greatest Purpose   0-8054-2323-0
God: The Enough   0-8054-2372-9
Prayer: The Greatest Power   0-8054-2349-4

Trusted
All Over the World

Daily Devotionals

Books and Videos

Day and Residential Courses

Counselling Training

Biblical Study Courses

Regional Seminars

Ministry to Women

CWR have been providing training and resources for Christians since the 1960s. From our headquarters at Waverley Abbey House we have been serving God's people with a vision to help apply God's Word to everyday life and relationships. The daily devotional *Every Day with Jesus* is read by over three-quarters of a million people in more than 150 countries, and our unique courses in biblical studies and pastoral care are respected all over the world.

For a free brochure about our seminars and courses or a catalogue of CWR resources please contact us at the following address:

CWR,
Waverley Abbey House,
Waverley Lane,
Farnham,
Surrey GU9 8EP

Telephone: 01252 784700
Email: mail@cwr.org.uk
Website: www.cwr.org.uk

CWR CRUSADE FOR WORLD REVIVAL *Applying God's Word to everyday life and relationship*